the bacon

cookbook

the bacon cookbook

More than 150 Recipes from Around the World for Everyone's Favorite Food

James Villas Photography by Andrea Grablewski

JOHN WILEY & SONS, INC.

Photography copyright © 2007 by Alexandra Grablewski

Published by John Wiley & Sons, Inc., Hoboken, New Jersey
Published simultaneously in Canada

Food styling by Cyd McDowell
Prop styling by Barb Fritz
Book design by Elizabeth Van Itallie

Library of Congress Cataloging-in-Publication Data:

Villas, James.
  The bacon cookbook / James Villas ; photography by Alexandra Grablewski.
    p. cm.
  Includes index.
  ISBN 978-0-470-04282-3
  1. Cookery (Bacon) I. Title.
  TX749.5.P67V55 2007
  641.6'64--dc22

                              2007007081

Printed in China

10 9 8 7 6 5 4 3 2

For Pamela Hoenig

Other Books by James Villas

American Taste, 1982

The Town & Country Cookbook, 1985

James Villas' Country Cooking, 1988

Villas at Table, 1988

The French Country Kitchen, 1992

My Mother's Southern Kitchen, 1994

Stews, Bogs, and Burgoos, 1997

My Mother's Southern Desserts, 1998

My Mother's Southern Entertaining, 2000

Between Bites, 2002

Crazy for Casseroles, 2003

Biscuit Bliss, 2004

Stalking the Green Fairy, 2004

The Glory of Southern Cooking, 2007

contents

preface

I don't hesitate a moment to proclaim bacon to be the greatest and most beloved food on earth. Most people, given good reason, can refuse a handful of salted nuts, dismiss a thick steak, or resist the temptation of rich chocolate cake. But who, under any circumstances, is not rendered almost helpless by the tantalizing sound of bacon sizzling slowly in a skillet, by the taunting backwoods aroma that permeates the air, by the luscious textures of crisp fat and toothsome lean meat, and by the explosion of mingled salty and smoky and sweet flavors that virtually explode in the mouth? Even staunch vegetarians, or those whose religious traditions forbid the consumption of any pork, are haunted instinctively by the sensuous, irresistible enticement of bacon, a gustatory seduction that extends to most cultures around the globe and has contributed substantially to the development and evolution of the world's foremost cuisines.

My own passionate love affair with bacon can be traced back to my earliest childhood days in North Carolina when, every Saturday morning without fail, the family would drive out to a working-farm market. There my mother and father would carefully inspect and select a couple of large streaky slabs destined to be thickly sliced and fried for a week's worth of hearty breakfasts. Also on the shopping agenda would be a chunk of lean cured salt pork ("streak-o'-lean") for seasoning boiled peas and vegetables, maybe some smoked jowl or bacon ends to be chopped and added to a savory poultry stew, and, when available, a cylinder of lean Canadian bacon intended either for the grill or for making sandwiches and salads. Since those nostalgic days, I must have consumed countless broiled chicken livers, olives, oysters, and dates wrapped in crispy bacon, some four or five thousand BLTs or bacon cheeseburgers, perhaps five hundred pounds of beans or peas seasoned with cured pork belly, and heaven knows how many tarts, soups, casseroles, roasted birds, and breads that depend on bacon or its succulent fat for their magic. And, yes indeed, at least four days a week I still fry up a couple of thick rashers to complement my normal breakfast eggs, fresh fruit, and biscuits.

While it's true that bacon is as American as fried chicken and apple pie, and that the variety and quality of most standard supermarket bacon seem to improve more each year, the majority of consumers are still unaware of not only the ever-growing number of premium artisanal bacons on the market but also the array of delectable foreign ones that are now available at specialty food outlets, online, and even in some supermarkets. Nor have American cooks (amateur and professional alike) paid that much attention to the multitude of neglected regional American bacon dishes, not to mention the large quantity of foreign ones that could add such engaging dimension to our repertory. Just the 40 percent increase in bacon consumption in the United States over the past five years might have justified my writing this book. But when I reflected on all the sumptuous bacon dishes I've tasted in my world travels over the years, it became obvious to me that what was really needed was not just a cookbook with contrived recipe variations on such familiar American classics as the BLT, Cobb salad, and baked beans, but one that was both fully regional and international in scope and authentic in context.

You'll find here, to be sure, plenty of bacon dips and canapés, all-American meat loaf and Louisiana Shrimp Creole, and French Quiche Lorraine and Italian Spaghetti alla Carbonara, but even more enticing are recipes for California Hangtown Fry, Iowa Bacon and Onion Casserole Bread, Swiss Potato and Bacon Cake, Irish Hot Pot, Philippine Adobo, Chinese Lion's Head, Ecuadorian Smoky Pumpkin Soup, and Portuguese Egg and Bacon Pudding. Throughout the book, I try to introduce you to the great bacons of the world and to utilize them in the appropriate dishes, but when this is not practical (or, in some cases, is impossible), I suggest alternatives that usually produce just as good results. One of the miracles of bacon is its easy adaptability to so many other foods, and while different cures and smoking techniques can have a pronounced effect on how much a certain bacon contributes to any given dish, I encourage you all along to experiment freely with various styles till you find the flavors and textures you prefer. Exotic new bacons are fascinating to eat and cook with, but quite honestly, it's rare that I've come upon a type for which there's not a sensible and satisfying substitute.

Today, there can be no question that the finest bacons (in America and elsewhere) are the old-fashioned styles produced by artisans obsessed with pigs raised in strict adherence to certain protocols of animal husbandry, with careful dry- or wet-curing procedures, and with long, painstaking smoking techniques that can spell the difference between superior and mediocre bacon. In this country alone, such fastidious champions as Bill Niman at Niman Ranch in California; Michael Zezzi and Jennifer Small at Flying Pigs Farm in upstate New York; Robert and James Nueske at Hillcrest Farm in Wisconsin; and veteran Velma Willett at Lazy H Smokehouse in Texas not only have revived many old-world production methods but are turning out dense, fragrant, woodsy, beautifully balanced bacons that can equal or surpass even the most highly respected European ones. And it's true that if all you've been accustomed to are certain mass-produced, vacuum-packed, quick-cured supermarket bacons that shrivel and curl pitifully in the skillet, exude a watery white liquid, and taste inordinately of chemicals, you'll be pleasantly stunned by many of the artisanal products available in some retail markets and on the Internet. (One California operation called The Grateful Palate has even formed a wildly successful online Bacon of the Month Club, where for about $140 plus shipping, connoisseurs are delivered a pound or so of different artisanal bacons each month.)

This is not to imply, by any means, that all expensive artisanal bacons are of the highest caliber and that all ordinary supermarket bacons are shoddy. On more than one occasion, I've ordered specialty bacons (domestic and foreign) that turned out to be discolored, disgustingly fatty, and tasteless, while, on the other hand, hardly a week passes that I don't encounter a familiar brand-name bacon (often on sale) that has just the right ratio of fat to lean, that is not too salty or smoky, that cooks perfectly soft or crisp, and that is packed with plenty of porky flavor. For this reason, you'll find that the recipes in this book call for just as much standard bacon as the artisanal variety, and as far as I'm concerned, anybody who balks at this viewpoint either makes no effort to study bacon carefully when shopping in the markets or is an unenlightened snob.

Another goal of this book is to squelch once and for all the erroneous and infuriating popular perception that bacon is a major culprit responsible for the ultimate nutritional demise of humanity. Yes, most bacon is relatively high in calories and sodium and fats (though devoid of any trans fat) and other components that make it taste so wonderful, but what the conscience-ridden fanatics fail to realize is that, compared with a single hot dog, a three-ounce hamburger, or a medium glazed doughnut, two or three slices of cooked bacon is almost a "health food." (Who cares to learn, for instance, that while two slices of cooked bacon contain about 73 calories, 202 milligrams of sodium, 6 grams of fat, and 11 milligrams of cholesterol, the comparative nutritive counts for one regular pork hot dog are a staggering 182 calories, 638 milligrams of sodium, 17 grams of fat, and 29 milligrams of cholesterol—plus the same sodium nitrite used as a preservative in bacon?) The problem, of course, is that most Americans have this frenzied compulsion (as in other eating habits) to consume four, six, even eight slices of bacon at a single sitting (my normal limit is two), then worry and complain about weight gain, elevated cholesterol, and heart disease. Heaven knows, I'm not one to preach when it comes to always eating wisely, but the truth is that devouring a quarter pound of luscious bacon at a time not only degrades the blissful pleasure but approaches sheer gluttony. As for cooking with bacon, if most of the recipes in this book illustrate nothing else, they prove that it takes very little bacon to transform numerous otherwise banal dishes into memorable culinary treasures.

"I've long said that if I were about to be executed and were given a choice of my last meal, it would be bacon and eggs," James Beard once wrote contemplatively. Under such dire circumstances, I must say I'd have to weigh my options carefully, but in all likelihood, I too would focus serious attention on this most earthy and heavenly of meats.

the international world of bacon

what is bacon?

Although defining bacon precisely is a complex matter involving different breeds of hogs and styles of animal husbandry, various international methods of butchery, and multiple production techniques, the term refers basically to the fatty meat from a pig's belly, side, back, and breast that is cured with salt and other preservatives and/or smoked. ("Fresh bacon"—usually from the belly—is neither cured nor smoked.) Today, the highest-quality bacon is made from hogs that are housed humanely, either fed a large percentage of barley and corn with no additives or left to root in fields, and slaughtered at certain weights.

Depending on the country of production, cured bacon is either left unsmoked (American salt pork and fatback, Italian pancetta, French *ventrèche,* Spanish *tocino*) or smoked for varying periods of time over hickory, applewood, oak, beech, and maple logs, chips, or sawdust, as well as over corncobs. After being cured and/or smoked, a side of streaky bacon (fat with even streaks of rosy lean meat) is either shipped to wholesale and retail butchers or divided into slabs or trimmed of rind and machine-sliced into three widths (thick, regular, and thin) before being distributed in vacuum-sealed packages. An average pound package of regular-sliced streaky bacon contains around eighteen to twenty $\frac{1}{16}$-inch-thick strips; thick-sliced contains about nine to twelve $\frac{1}{8}$-inch-thick strips.

Just as real hamburgers are not made with chicken, nor martinis with vodka, genuine bacon is not made with beef, turkey, or duck.

a short history of bacon

Bacon is one of the oldest meats in history, and while there are multiple and conflicting theories dating its origins, it is generally believed that the Chinese were the first to develop a method of salting and preserving pork bellies as early as 1500 B.C. In ancient Greece, the fabulist Aesop referred to bacon in 550 B.C., and by the first century A.D. of the Roman Empire, the cured meat had become such a basic food for the poor that special hogs in the region of Lucania were being bred exclusively to meet the large demand. (When the Roman epicure Apicius compiled the first known cookbook during this period, he included a recipe for pork that was to be salted for seventeen days, air-dried for two days, then smoked two days longer—a technique not unlike those used for producing some bacons today.)

In England, beans and bacon were common fare for the poor throughout the Middle Ages, while, in stark contrast, one of the most ceremonial aristocratic events in France was a feast termed *le repas bakonique* that featured only pork dishes. At about the same time, Germanic peoples were eating a smoked pork product known as *bakkon,* and by the Elizabethan era back in England, *bakoun,* or bacon, cured with a new compound called saltpeter (potassium nitrate), began to assume the basic form and flavor we know today. (The phrase "to bring home the bacon" supposedly alludes to an old rural English tradition whereby a flitch, or side, of bacon was offered as a prize to any man who could swear before the church that for a year and a day he had neither quarreled with his wife nor wished himself single.) All that remained was for an enterprising farmer in Wiltshire by the name of John Harris to establish the first large-scale bacon-curing operation during England's Industrial Revolution in the late eighteenth century, and for the next two hundred years, Wiltshire bacon remained the standard by which all other styles were judged.

There can be little doubt that bacon was in the larder (a term derived from the Latin word for bacon fat) of the *Mayflower* when the first Pilgrims came to America in 1620, and we know from early cookbooks that the cured bellies and backs of hogs were not only a popular, economical staple in the Colonial diet but also the ideal ingredients for flavoring dozens of soups, stews, and otherwise bland, starchy dishes.

Westward expansion in the nineteenth century would have been almost inconceivable without literally thousands of pounds of preserved bacon to feed explorers, prospectors, and settlers and to be rendered into lard for frying fish and potatoes and making biscuits. It's been conjectured that one reason the South lost the Civil War was because strategic cured pork rations dwindled to the point where Confederate troops were half-starved. And perhaps never did bacon play a more vital role in human survival than during the twentieth century's Great Depression, when millions of impoverished Americans depended on the nourishing, inexpensive meat to sustain them through one of the most wretched chapters of our history.

Most of today's dynamic bacon industry in the United States (and elsewhere) can be traced back to three early-twentieth-century Midwestern meat packers: Philip D. Armour, Gustavus F. Swift, and, above all, Oscar F. Mayer. Armour and Swift improved methods of meat preservation and built the first refrigerated railroad cars to transport large quantities of processed hogs from Chicago slaughterhouses to retail butchers, but it was the German immigrant Mayer who, in the 1920s, perfected a method of slicing and packaging bacon that would revolutionize the industry worldwide. After the innovations of these pioneers, it was only a matter of time before artisans from Wisconsin to New Hampshire to Kentucky exploited old-world curing and smoking traditions combined with modern domestic technology to create some of the finest bacons on earth.

the curing and smoking of bacon

For centuries, pork has been transformed into bacon by curing the pig belly, flank, upper back, and other fatty cuts of meat with salt and other preservative agents. Today, the very finest (and most expensive) bacon is still traditionally dry-cured by small artisanal producers, who rub the slabs of meat with a dry mixture of salt, sugar, and seasonings, with several sodium compounds included as preservatives and flavorings, then hang them a week or so to dry naturally and intensify their succulence. Other artisanal and most larger commercial producers wet-cure the meat in brine for up to twenty-four hours, add to the solution not only sodium nitrite and nitrate to prevent spoilage and enhance color but also any number of distinctive seasonings (brown sugar, maple syrup, honey, paprika, spices, and the like), and hang the slabs for up to a week. In the United States and some other countries, mass-produced and less distinguished brands of bacon are injected with a saline solution and cured no longer than a few hours to speed up the process and add bulk, which is why some bacons exude a watery, white liquid when cooked. (Since nitrites and nitrates are suspected to be carcinogenic in large amounts, the USDA regulates their use in the production of all bacon and other foods in the United States. A few American producers do cure bacon that contains no chemicals, but since nitrites and nitrates help the even penetration of salt throughout the raw meat and provide much of the characteristic bacon flavor and rosy color, this bacon is generally brown in color, insipid, and tastes more like roast pork.)

Certain styles of Portuguese *toucinho,* German *Speck,* northern Italian *Speck Alto Adige,* and Chinese bacon are rubbed with salt and various seasonings, then air-cured naturally from seven to ten days. These bacons may or may not be smoked for enhanced flavor.

Virtually all bacon is cured in some way, but not all bacon is smoked. If cured caringly, unsmoked bacon can be delicious, but the real key to most superior bacon lies not in the curing lockers or tanks but in the way it is smoked. Smoking not only imparts more flavor to the bacon but also enhances the curing process and renders some of the fat. Smoking methods vary enormously from one craftsman to the next, but most American and European artisanal producers smoke their cured sides of bacon naturally and slowly in smokehouses over wood logs or chips (hickory, applewood, oak, cherry, maple, beech) or dried corncobs, a time-consuming technique that can last up to a week or longer for double-smoked bacons. Giant commercial companies can either smoke their bacons with sawdust in stainless-steel smokers for four to six hours or simply inject the meat with liquid smoke. Since long smoking partially cooks bacon and reduces its fat content, a pound of raw artisanal bacon yields about three-quarters of a pound of cooked, whereas more ordinary, quick-smoked bacon produces as little as a quarter to a third. The ideal result of long, careful smoking is a dense bacon with firm, smooth fat and dark pink to mahogany lean meat; one that does not shrink excessively in the frying pan; and one that delivers just the right rich balance of meat and crackling fat and a mellow smoky flavor.

international styles of bacon

AMERICA

SLAB BACON: A whole cured and/or smoked slab of pork belly with rind and streaks of lean meat. The average ratio is about two-thirds fat to one-third lean meat. Lightly smoked to double-smoked for more intense flavor. Available in most markets and online from artisanal producers.

STREAKY BACON: Slab bacon that is either left whole or trimmed of rind, sliced, and then packaged as thin-sliced, regular-sliced ($\frac{1}{16}$-inch-thick), and thick-sliced ($\frac{1}{8}$-inch-thick). The most common style of sliced bacon available in all markets and online from artisanal producers.

COUNTRY-STYLE BACON: Cured, salty, heavily smoked bacon produced from the same hogs bred for Smithfield and other country hams. Often available at specialty butchers and food markets. The term can also refer to any bacon that is sliced thickly.

DOUBLE-SMOKED BACON: Cured slab or streaky bacon smoked up to twenty-four hours for more pungent flavor and less shrinkage. Much darker fat and lean meat. Used mainly for flavoring in cooking. Available in some supermarkets and online from some artisanal producers.

SALT PORK: Cured, unsmoked fat from pig belly or side that can include a little lean meat. Also called "white bacon" and "streak-o'-lean." Used mainly for flavoring in cooking and rendering into crisp cracklings. Available sealed in plastic packages in most markets.

FATBACK: Fresh, uncured, unsmoked fat from pig back; used for flavoring in cooking and making lard. Not the same as salt pork. Available sealed in plastic packages in many markets.

JOWL: Boneless, cured, smoked pig cheek that is fatter than streaky bacon and either eaten fried or used for flavoring in cooking. Available mostly in Southern markets and in specialty butcher shops.

CANADIAN-STYLE BACON: Lean, cured, lightly smoked, and precooked eye of pig loin that is widely marketed in packaged cylinders and resembles ham more than bacon. Known only as "back bacon" in Canada, and not to be confused with authentic, unsmoked Canadian peameal bacon. Widely available.

BACON BITS: Crisp pieces of slab or streaky bacon that are preserved, dried, and used in tossed salads, soups, and casseroles. (Vegetable-based imitation bacon bits are also available in jars but are not recommended.)

GREAT BRITAIN

ENGLISH BACON: Lean, meaty, cured, and/or smoked lower pig loin with a "tail," or ring, of fat. Known as "back bacon" in the United Kingdom. Small selection available in finer supermarkets and online.

IRISH BACON: Basically the same as English bacon but often saltier and more heavily smoked. Small selection available in finer supermarkets and online.

STREAKY BACON: Same as American streaky bacon but generally with more lean meat.

COLLAR BACON: Cured, smoked pig upper back (near head) that is more fatty than English or Irish bacon. Sometimes available at specialty butchers.

WILTSHIRE BACON: Lean, brine-cured, oak-smoked bacon cut from the center backs of special saddleback pigs. Considered by connoisseurs to be the sweetest and finest British bacon. Available online.

GAMMON: Cured, smoked bacon cut from pig's upper hind legs before the legs are removed from carcass and cured as ham (also called gammon). Unavailable outside of Great Britain.

CANADA

PEAMEAL BACON: Authentic lean "Canadian bacon" cut from the eye of the pig loin; sweet-pickle-cured, unsmoked, and coated in peameal or yellow cornmeal. Available online in slabs or slices.

BACK BACON: Same as American "Canadian-style bacon."

FRANCE

LARD SALÉ: Cured slab of pig belly with or without streaks of lean meat; used mainly in cooking and particularly for the popular bistro dish *petit salé* (salt pork with lentils). Similar to American salt pork but saltier and often requires preblanching. Available online.

LARD FUMÉ: Cured and/or smoked slab of pig belly; similar to American slab bacon and used mainly in cooking. Available online.

VENTRÈCHE: Cured, unsmoked, rolled pig belly or breast; used mainly in cooking. Similar to Italian pancetta. Available online.

COUENNE: Rind from a slab of *lard salé* or *lard fumé;* used exclusively to flavor soups and stews.

LARDONS: Diced *lard salé* or *lard fumé;* used mainly in cooking and, rendered till crisp, for salads.

ITALY

PANCETTA (IMPORTED AND DOMESTIC): Dry-cured, unsmoked, spiced, dry-aged pig belly with streaks of lean meat; used mainly for flavoring in cooking. Widely available in cased rolls or sliced and packaged in plastic. Keeps up to three months in plastic in the refrigerator.

PANCETTA AFFUMICATA: Smoked pancetta popular in northeastern Italy and similar to American streaky bacon. Available in slabs and slices in Italian markets and in slabs online.

GUANCIALE: Dry-cured and smoked pig jowl and cheek popular in southern Italy and used mainly in cooking. Available in some Italian markets and online in cased rolls.

RIGATINO: Lean pancetta from Tuscany produced from free-range pigs. Available in some Italian markets.

LARDO: Dense, white, delicate fat from pig rump cured for months with salt, spices, and herbs and served raw paper-thin on toasted bread. Available in some Italian markets and online.

SPECK ALTO ADIGE: Lean, cured, juniper-smoked, air-dried pig leg that is a specialty of Italy's most northern province. Eaten raw or used in cooking as a smoky alternative to pancetta.

SPAIN

TOCINO: Pig belly cured in a special storage of salt crystals and used exclusively in cooking. Not available in the United States. Best American substitute is salt pork with no lean streaks.

"BACON": Cured, smoked pig belly similar to American streaky bacon.

PORTUGAL

TOUCINHO: Pig belly that is either dry-cured and smoked or air-cured. Produced in northern Portugal from pigs fed chestnuts and potatoes. Not available in the United States. Best American substitute is slab bacon with lean streaks.

GERMANY, AUSTRIA, AND SWITZERLAND

SPECK: Cured, heavily smoked, air-dried pig belly or side that is eaten fried or used in cooking. Available in slabs or slices at German butchers and delis or online. Best American substitute is double-smoked slab or streaky bacon.

GERÄUCHERTER SPECK: Cured, mellow pig belly or breast that is double-smoked over beechwood. An East Prussian specialty available at German butchers and online.

PAPRIKASPECK: Cured, smoked pig belly heavily seasoned with paprika. A specialty of Westphalia. Available at some German butchers and online.

BAUCHSPECK: Air-cured, birch-smoked pig belly popular in southern Switzerland and southwestern Austria. Rarely available in the United States.

SWARTZWÄLDERSPECK (BLACK FOREST BACON): Cured, smoked, cooked pig belly with streaks of lean meat; eaten as is or used in cooking throughout the Baden region of Germany. Available in most German delis and specialty food shops.

HUNGARY

PAPRIKA BACON: Dry-cured pig belly or neck soaked in a paprika solution, dried three to four days, smoked fifteen to twenty hours, and eaten cooked or used in cooking. Available in Hungarian and German markets and online.

CORNED BACON: Dry-cured pig belly or neck soaked in a garlic saline solution for five days, smoked till mahogany in color, and used mainly in cooking. Available in Hungarian markets and online.

GARLIC BACON: Pig belly soaked in a garlic saline solution for five days, dry-cured in salt, coated with beef blood and paprika, and heavily smoked to dry-burn the coating. Used mainly in cooking. Available in Hungarian markets and online.

GYPSY BACON: Cured, spiced pig belly blackened with pig's blood before long smoking. Eaten uncooked or cooked. Available at Hungarian markets, some specialty food shops, and online.

DENMARK

DANISH BACON: Lean, cured, smoked slab or streaky bacon cut from the backs of special Landrace pigs. Similar to English and Irish "back bacon" but saltier. Available online.

BROWN SUGAR SLAB BACON: Very lean, brown-sugar-cured, smoked pig upper belly or tenderloin prized by bacon connoisseurs. Available in large slabs online.

CHINA

LOP YUK (CHINESE BACON): Pig belly that is either air-cured with soy sauce, brown sugar, and spices for seven to ten days till mellow and very hard, or cured for four days, then smoked about five hours. Must be soaked for at least six hours before being sliced and fried or chopped; used for flavoring numerous Chinese dishes.

Available in long, stringed pieces in Chinese markets and online. Also available in most Chinese markets is fresh, soft, uncured slab pig belly; used as a main ingredient in certain Chinese dishes.

buying bacon

Whether you're shopping for streaky bacon slices (or rashers); slab bacon; lean Canadian, British, or Danish bacon; or an exotic Hungarian or Chinese one, careful inspection can mean the difference between supreme satisfaction and gloomy disappointment. For regular slices of cured and/or smoked bacon, I don't hesitate a second to ask a butcher or clerk to hold up a slice or two or rummage finickily through prepackaged stacks in supermarkets, rejecting any that does not have an almost equal ratio of fat to lean meat or is off-color. The color and texture of bacon depends on how (and for how long) it was cured and smoked, but generally the fat should be firm and pure white to pale golden, and the lean, from bright pink to reddish-brown. Remember that the firmer the fat, the less the sliced bacon will curl as it cooks; likewise, although the thinner the bacon the crisper it will be when cooked, the most serious artisanal producers prefer to thick-cut their bacon for the richest texture.

Slab bacon comes in one whole piece, including its rind, it keeps longer in the refrigerator than precut slices, and it's often the best choice when you prefer to cut your own strips a certain width or need chunks and pieces of bacon for cooking. (Slab bacon can also be significantly cheaper than sliced.) The same standards of fat-to-lean ratio, texture, and color for sliced bacon apply to slab bacon—though slabs of certain Hungarian and German bacons can be considerably darker than other styles, depending on cures and smoking techniques. Salt pork (with or without streaks of lean meat), fatback, jowl, and French *lard salé* are also marketed mainly in slabs, and never is it more important that the fat in these cooking bacons be pristine. The same holds true for domestic and imported rolls of Italian pancetta, which should have an equal ratio of glistening white fat and bright pink lean meat.

Today, genuine English, Irish, and Danish back bacon can be ordered online from any number of distributors (see Mail-Order Sources for Premium Bacons, p. 17), and a small selection of these same bacons is increasingly available in specialty food shops and high-end supermarkets. Cut partly from the pig loin, these bacons should typically display a large section of lean meat either that is surrounded by a thin ring of white fat or to which a "tail" of fat is connected. Closely related but cut exclusively from the lean loin, most Canadian-style bacon (known only as peameal or back bacon in

Canada) is produced and marketed widely in the United States.

Air-cured Chinese bacon can be ordered online, but to be absolutely certain what you're buying, you're almost obliged to visit a Chinese market—or, as I've done, ask the friendly owner of a reliable Chinese restaurant to sell you a long, narrow piece. Genuine Chinese bacon is traditionally cured on a string, very dark in color, and always hard as a rock. Rarely will you find any that has already been soaked in water, rehydrated, and ready to use, though there might be fresh, uncured pig belly in some markets.

Remember that any packaged bacon should be purchased before the "sell by" date printed on the package. This does not necessarily mean that the bacon should not be consumed after that date (most packaged bacon, once opened, will remain fresh in the refrigerator at least a week), only that the producer has told the market to remove the bacon from the shelf after the "pull" date.

Artisanal and foreign bacons (both those found in better markets and the ones ordered online) can be about double the price of ordinary supermarket bacon and are generally worth the extra cost. There is never any guarantee, however, that the more expensive bacons are automatically better than the mass-produced ones, and while I'm forever encountering discolored, excessively fatty, disgraceful brands stacked high in even the most reputable supermarkets, I do find (often on sale) regular American bacons that are equal or superior in quality to even the most acclaimed and sought-after varieties. The smart consumer learns to recognize what fine bacon looks like, experiments with different types and brands, and refuses to pay high prices for shoddy products.

storing bacon

Vacuum-sealed sliced bacon remains fresh in the refrigerator for several weeks after the "sell by" date stamped on the package, but once the bacon is opened, it should be kept in airtight plastic bags in the coldest area of the refrigerator and consumed within 1 or 2 weeks. Since opened slab bacon has less surface area susceptible to air and bacteria, it will keep well in airtight plastic up to about 3 weeks. If the lean meat of any bacon darkens noticeably and the fat stiffens, this is a sign that the bacon is becoming rancid. Naturally smoked bacons tend to maintain their integrity longer than unsmoked or artificially soaked ones. Unsoaked, hard Chinese bacon wrapped in plastic can be stored almost indefinitely in the refrigerator.

Because of its high salt and fat content, bacon does not lend itself well to long freezing—even when vacuum-sealed or in airtight freezer bags—and I personally never freeze any sliced bacon. Carefully wrapped in foil and/or freezer bags, slab bacon, salt pork, rolls of pancetta, and most Hungarian bacons may be frozen up to a month or so without losing much moisture, turning hard, and tasting rancid. (Rancid bacon is not harmful; it just tastes wretched.) To defrost bacon, submerge the container in luke-warm water for about ten minutes.

Since bacon does not generally store well for long periods, the best overall advice is to buy no more than a week's supply at a time.

cooking bacon

TO FRY: Arrange slices of streaky bacon side by side in an unheated heavy skillet (or cut them in half crosswise to better accommodate the size of the skillet) and fry over moderate to moderately low heat till the desired crispness, 8 to 15 minutes, turning once or twice with a fork. (I personally believe that bacon cooked too crispy loses most of its meltingly chewy quality.) The lower the heat, the less curling, shrinking, and chance of burning. (Most ordinary supermarket bacon, injected with liquid curing agents, shrivels in the skillet more than dry-cured artisanal bacon.) Drain the bacon on paper towels and reserve the fat in a clean coffee can or other container to use for fry-ing and flavoring other foods.

TO BROIL: Preheat the oven broiler. Arrange slices of streaky bacon side by side on a slotted broiler rack set over a broiler pan and broil about 3 to 4 inches from the heat till the desired crispness, 6 to 10 minutes, turning the slices once with a fork and watching carefully to avoid burning. Drain the bacon on paper towels and reserve the fat in a clean coffee can or other container to use for frying and flavoring other foods. (Broiling is the most convenient way to cook large quantities of bacon.)

TO BAKE: Preheat the oven to 350°F. Arrange slices of streaky bacon slightly overlap-ping on a slotted broiler rack set over a broiler pan and bake in the upper third of the oven till nicely browned, 15 to 20 minutes, never turning. Drain the bacon on paper towels and reserve the fat in a coffee can or other container to use for frying or flavor-ing other foods. (Baking is a good method to cook thick-cut bacon slices not intended to be as crisp as fried or broiled bacon.)

TO MICROWAVE: Arrange slices of streaky bacon side by side on a microwave rack over a microwave dish, cover with several layers of paper towels, and cook on high heat about 1 minute per slice. Otherwise, arrange slices of bacon side by side between several layers of paper towels on a microwave plate and cook on high about 1 minute per slice. (No doubt microwave bacon is quick and easy, but I never use this method since the bacon can become dry and hard before you realize it.)

TO BLANCH DICED SLAB BACON OR SALT PORK: Place the diced meat in a heavy skillet or saucepan with enough water to cover and bring to a boil. Reduce the heat to moderately low, simmer about 3 minutes, and drain the meat on paper towels. (To make *lardons* for salads, drain the water from the skillet or pan, stir the pieces of meat till browned and crisp, 8 to 10 minutes, and drain on paper towels.)

saving and cooking with bacon fat

Small amounts of rendered bacon fat are useful (and often indispensable) not only for enhancing all sorts of international soups, stews, vegetables, casseroles, and other dishes but also for cooking such items as fried chicken, seafood, and apples, greens for hot salads, and certain pasta and rice preparations. Save bacon fat in a clean coffee can or other container and keep tightly covered at room temperature up to 1 month or till the can is about half-full. To keep the fat from turning rancid, transfer it to a saucepan, add a few tablespoons of water, and sprinkle about 1 tablespoon of flour over the top (to help any sediment to settle). Slowly bring to a boil, remove from the heat to cool slightly, and strain through cheesecloth into another clean container. Let cool completely, cover tightly, and store in the refrigerator. The fat rendered from heavily salted, processed bacon will keep much longer than that from nitrite-free organic bacon. If, at any time, bacon fat tastes or smells rancid, discard it and begin a new container. (Never add any other rendered meat or poultry fat to a container of bacon fat.)

bacon and health

While bacon contains no trans fat and is a source of vitamins, protein, niacin, potassium, zinc, and selenium, it's no secret to anyone that it is also high in sodium, total fat, and cholesterol, and that most bacon, like many other meats, is processed with potentially carcinogenic nitrites and nitrates for preservation, flavor, and color. One cooked slice of streaky bacon contains between 35 and 40 calories, 100 milligrams of sodium, and about 3 grams of fat (but, again, no trans fat), depending on the percentage of lean meat. Yet an average slice has about one-quarter fewer calories than a tablespoon of butter or margarine, roughly half the total fat, and almost three times less cholesterol than butter. (Rendered bacon fat has considerably more calories, fat, and cholesterol, but since normally only small amounts are used for flavoring dishes, the nutritive counts are virtually negligible.) Those overly concerned about sodium content in bacon now have more and more options to purchase low-sodium alternatives, and although nitrites and nitrates in all cured meat products are carefully controlled by the USDA, chemical-free bacons are increasingly available to wary consumers willing to compromise flavor and long shelf life.

mail-order sources for premium bacons

In addition to the wide variety of standard, mass-produced cured and/or smoked bacons, many supermarkets and retail food shops are now stocking more and more domestic and foreign artisanal products destined for the most discerning customers. To order by phone or online some of the finest premium bacons available in this country, contact the following sources. (Average prices range from about $7.50 to $10.50 per pound, plus shipping.)

BENTON'S SMOKY MOUNTAIN COUNTRY HAMS (Madisonville, Tennessee): 1-423-442-5003; www.bentonshams.com. Hickory-smoked bacon.

BURGERS' SMOKEHOUSE (California, Missouri): 1-800-345-5185; www.smokehouse.com. Country air-cured, hickory-smoked bacon, peppered bacon, and country ham bacon.

D'ARTAGNAN (Newark, New Jersey): 1-800-327-8246; www.dartnagnan.com. Large selection of domestic artisanal bacons, *ventrèche,* pancetta, *Speck Alto Adige,* and nitrite-free smoked bacon.

FLYING PIGS FARM (Shushan, New York): 1-518-854-3844; www.flyingpigsfarm.com. Smoked slab bacon, streaky bacon, and Canadian-style bacon produced from special heritage hogs. Also fresh belly and nitrate-free slab and streaky bacon.

THE GRATEFUL PALATE (Oxnard, California): 1-888-472-5283; www.gratefulpalate.com. Features Bacon of the Month Club: a different artisanal bacon delivered every month ($140 per year plus shipping and handling).

IGOURMET.COM (northeast Pennsylvania): 1-877-446-8763; www.igourmet.com. Brown-sugar-cured bacon, applewood-smoked bacon, Irish and Danish back bacon, pancetta, *ventrèche,* and *Speck Alto Adige.*

KAM MAN FOOD PRODUCTS (New York, New York): 1-212-571-0330; www.kammanfood.com. Chinese bacon.

LAZY H SMOKEHOUSE (Kirbyville, Texas): 1-409-423-3309. Naturally oak-smoked bacon produced from special Texas hogs. No preservatives, no additives.

MCARTHUR'S SMOKEHOUSE (Charlottesville, Virginia): 1-800-382-8177; www.finefoodnow.com. Applewood- and hickory-smoked bacon and Canadian-style bacon.

NEWSOM'S OLD MILL STORE (Princeton, Kentucky): 1-270-365-2482; www.newsomscountryham.com. Hickory-smoked bacon, peppered bacon, and nitrite-free bacon.

NIMAN RANCH (Oakland, California): 1-866-808-0340; www.nimanranch.com. Cured and uncured applewood-smoked bacon, pancetta, and guanciale. All-natural bacon produced from free-range pigs fed only the finest grains; with no hormones or antibiotics. Streaky bacon also available in select specialty food shops and super-markets.

NODINE'S SMOKEHOUSE (Torrington, Connecticut): 1-800-222-2059; www.nodinesmokehouse.com. Applewood-smoked slab and streaky bacon, double-smoked bacon, juniper bacon, garlic bacon, peppered bacon, Canadian-style bacon, and Irish back bacon. Some products available in select New York City, Connecticut, Kentucky, and Massachusetts retail markets.

NORTH COUNTRY SMOKEHOUSE (Claremont, New Hampshire): 1-800-258-4304; www.ncsmokehouse.com. Applewood-, maple-, and cob-smoked slab and streaky bacon, peppered bacon, and Canadian-style bacon.

NUESKE'S HILLCREST FARM (Wittenberg, Wisconsin): 1-800-392-2266; www.nueske.com. Applewood-smoked slab and streaky bacon. Also available in some retail markets.

OZARK MOUNTAIN SMOKEHOUSE (Branson, Missouri): 1-800-643-3437. Dry-cured, hickory-smoked slab and streaky bacon, peppered bacon, Canadian-style bacon, and special "Arkansas bacon" (cut from pig's upper shoulder).

THE REAL CANADIAN BACON COMPANY (Troy, Michigan): 1-800-222-6601; www.realcanadianbacon.com. Genuine Canadian peameal bacon.

SALUMERIA BIELLESE (New York, New York): 1-212-736-7376; www.salumeriabiellese.com. Domestic pancetta, guanciale, and lardo.

SCHALLER & WEBER (New York, New York): 1-212-879-3047; www.schallerweber.com. Black Forest regular and double-smoked bacon, Irish back bacon, and Hungarian rib bacon.

S. WALLACE EDWARDS & SONS (Surry, Virginia): 1-800-222-4267; www.virginiatraditions.com. Brown-sugar-, dry-cured, hickory-smoked bacon and peppered bacon.

VERMONT SMOKE & CURE (South Barre, Vermont): 1-802-476-4666. Maple-cured bacon and cob-smoked bacon.

WILLIAM'S (Lumberton, North Carolina): 1-910-608-2226; www.britishbacon.com. English Wiltshire bacon and Irish back bacon.

YORKVILLE PACKING HOUSE (New York, New York): 1-212-628-5147; www.hungarianmeatmarket.com. Large selection of Eastern European bacons, including double-smoked farmer's bacon, Hungarian gypsy bacon, paprika bacon, and deep-fried cracklings.

canapés and appetizers

Bacon and Shrimp Fingers
Spicy Chicken Livers in Blankets
Horseradish Mussels and Bacon
Bacon, Peanut Butter, and Scallion Canapés
Guacamole and Bacon Canapés
Lacquered Chinese Bacon
Bacon-Banana Treats
Bacon, Cream Cheese, and Horseradish Dip
Hot Bacon–Blue Cheese Dip
Bacon-Almond Cheese Spread
Bacon-Cheddar Popcorn
Bacon-Stuffed Cremini Mushrooms
Clams Casino
Bacon-Wrapped Dungeness Crab Legs
French Cheese and Bacon Puffs
Devils on Horseback
Grilled Bacon-Wrapped Date Tapas
French Country Pâté
Japanese Bacon Tempura
Pancetta and Mozzarella Pizzas

bacon and shrimp fingers

Peppered bacon adds a pleasant zing to these fingers, but you could also use a spicy Italian pancetta or Hungarian paprika bacon. Just make sure the bacon has a reasonable amount of lean meat in proportion to fat.

9 slices lean peppered bacon, cut in half
½ pound fresh shrimp
¼ cup tomato juice
1 large egg
½ cup fine dry bread crumbs
1 tablespoon finely chopped parsley leaves
1 tablespoon fresh lemon juice
½ teaspoon Worcestershire sauce
¼ teaspoon salt
Freshly ground black pepper to taste

- In a large skillet, fry the bacon till half-cooked and drain on paper towels.
- Place the shrimp in a saucepan with enough water to cover, bring to a boil, remove from the heat, and let stand 2 minutes. Drain the shrimp, peel and devein, and chop finely.
- Preheat the oven broiler.
- In a mixing bowl, whisk together the tomato juice and egg till well blended, add the chopped shrimp and remaining ingredients, and mix thoroughly with your hands till the mixture is tightened, adding a few more bread crumbs if necessary. Roll equal parts of the mixture into 18 fingers, wrap each finger with a piece of bacon, and secure with toothpicks soaked in water. Place on the rack of a broiling pan and broil about 4 inches from the heat till the bacon is crisp, 5 to 6 minutes, turning once. Serve hot or at room temperature as a canapé.

MAKES 18 FINGERS

spicy chicken livers in blankets

Bacon has an affinity with virtually all types of liver, and even those who shy away from mild chicken livers will become hooked on the many complex flavors of these spicy canapés. If the livers appear too big to be popped into the mouth in a single bite, cut them in half before wrapping in bacon. Also, the bacon slices should not be too thick.

½ cup all-purpose flour
½ teaspoon powdered sage
¼ teaspoon cayenne pepper
Salt to taste
1 pound chicken livers, rinsed and patted dry
8 to 9 slices lean maple-smoked bacon, cut in half crosswise
½ cup vegetable oil

- In a small bowl, combine the flour, sage, cayenne, and salt and stir till well blended. Dredge the livers in the seasoned flour, wrap each with a piece of bacon, and secure with toothpicks soaked in water. Dredge lightly again in the flour and set aside.

- In a large, heavy skillet, heat the oil over moderate heat, add the livers, and cook, turning once, till they are just cooked through and the bacon is crisp, 8 to 9 minutes in all. Drain on paper towels and serve immediately.

MAKES 16 TO 18 CANAPÉS

BACON BONUS
To prevent packaged bacon slices from tearing, let stand about 15 minutes at room temperature before peeling them off.

horseradish mussels and bacon

These tangy mussels are unusual and delicious either passed as canapés or served as an appetizer. They can also be just as easily secured with toothpicks soaked in water and fried (with no extra fat added to the skillet) 3 to 4 minutes, then garnished with sprigs of rosemary. Whichever method you choose, just remember that mussels toughen quickly from overcooking. Ordinary cured supermarket bacon is fully acceptable for this dish.

18 slices streaky bacon, cut in half
36 fresh mussels in the shells
1 to 2 cups water
1 cup fine dry bread crumbs
½ cup prepared horseradish
Sprigs of fresh rosemary, part of leaves stripped

• In a large skillet, fry the bacon over moderate heat till half-cooked, drain on paper towels, and cut in half.

• Scrub the mussels well with a stiff brush, rinse, and place in a large kettle with the water. Bring the water to a boil, reduce the heat to moderately low, cover, and steam till the shells open, about 10 minutes (discard any that do not open). When cool enough to handle, pry the mussels from the shells with a heavy knife, reserving as much of the liquor as possible in a bowl. Trim away any stray whiskers on the mussels and strain the liquor through cheesecloth into another bowl.

• Preheat the oven to 400°F.

• On a plate, combine the bread crumbs, horseradish, and reserved mussel liquor and stir till well blended and pasty. Dredge each mussel lightly in the mixture, then press the mixture firmly on the mussels with your fingers. Wrap each mussel with half a slice of bacon, secure each with a sprig of rosemary, and bake till the bacon is crispy, about 8 minutes. Serve hot.

MAKES 36 CANAPÉS

bacon, peanut butter, and scallion canapés

Only Americans (including children) appreciate the close affinity of peanut butter and bacon, and while nothing is better for lunch than an ordinary peanut butter and bacon sandwich on white, upgrade the combination with a few scallions, Worcestershire, and brown sugar and you have small hot canapés that are perfect for a bridge luncheon or afternoon tea. While you can use regular cured bacon, here's a good chance to try a mellow maple-smoked artisanal one or, if you can locate it, a honey-cured bacon.

6 slices lean maple-smoked bacon, cut into 1½-inch pieces
½ cup smooth peanut butter
4 scallions (white parts only), minced
2 tablespoons lemon juice
2 teaspoons Worcestershire sauce
3 tablespoons mayonnaise
1 teaspoon light brown sugar
9 slices whole-grain bread, crusts removed

• Preheat the oven to 400°F.

• In a large skillet, fry the bacon pieces over moderate heat till almost crisp and drain on paper towels.

• In a small bowl, combine the peanut butter, scallions, lemon juice, Worcestershire, 1 tablespoon of the mayonnaise, and brown sugar and stir till well blended.

• Spread the remaining 2 tablespoons mayonnaise lightly over the bread slices and spread equal amounts of the peanut butter mixture over the slices. Cut the slices into quarters and arrange on a baking sheet. Place a piece of bacon on top of each canapé and bake till the bacon is fully crisp, about 10 minutes. Serve hot or at room temperature.

MAKES 36 CANAPÉS

guacamole and bacon canapés

Derived from the ancient Mexican word for avocado mixture or sauce (*ahua-camolli*), *guacamole* refers to a popular appetizer throughout central Mexico that is often enhanced either by dried bits of fried pork skin called *chicharrón* or by crumbled bacon. Traditionally, guacamole is prepared in a three-legged stone mortar (*molcajete*) and served with tortillas or corn chips, but I've discovered it's also very good when spread on thin, buttered pumpernickel slices as a canapé. Do remember that guacamole should always be more chunky than smooth. Also, if you need to chill the mixture more than 20 minutes, add the avocado seed to the mixture to prevent darkening.

1 ripe avocado, peeled and seeded
½ small ripe tomato, chopped
3 tablespoons minced scallions (white parts only)
1 tablespoon minced fresh coriander (cilantro) leaves
1 small chile pepper, minced
1 tablespoon fresh lime juice
Salt and freshly ground black pepper to taste
8 slices lean slab bacon
12 thin slices pumpernickel bread, crusts removed
Softened butter for spreading

• In a bowl, mash the avocado with a wooden spoon till lumpy, add the tomato, scallions, coriander, chile pepper, lime juice, and salt and pepper, and mix till well blended. Cover the guacamole with plastic wrap and chill briefly.

• In a large skillet, fry the bacon over moderate heat till crisp, drain on paper towels, and crumble. Add the bacon to the guacamole and stir till well blended.

• Lightly butter the bread slices, spread the guacamole equally on the slices, and cut into thirds.

MAKES 36 CANAPÉS

lacquered chinese bacon

Air-cured with sugar, soy sauce, and spices, Chinese bacon is the ancestor of all bacon, has a distinctive sweet flavor like none other, and is used to flavor numerous Chinese dishes. No doubt this particular lacquered bacon is a Chinese-American creation, and I first encountered it at the lavish private receptions once thrown at a now-gone restaurant in New York City called Mortimer's. Chinese bacon is available at most Asian markets and online (most often in long, hard pieces), but if you're unable to find it, substitute a good applewood- or maple-smoked artisanal slab bacon. (Thick-cut slices of any streaky bacon can also be prepared in this manner.) Since these bacon pieces disappear at parties faster than you can pass them, I strongly suggest you make plenty. Stored in an airtight container, the pieces keep well for a couple of days and make a great snack.

1-pound piece air-dried Chinese bacon, soaked in water at least 6 hours
1½ cups light brown sugar

- Preheat the oven to 425°F.
- With a sharp, heavy knife, remove and discard the rind of the bacon and cut the meat crosswise into ⅛-inch-thick pieces. Place the sugar in a wide dish and dredge both sides of each bacon piece in the sugar, pressing the sugar firmly onto the pieces with your fingers. Arrange the slices on the rack of a broiling pan and bake, turning once, till the bacon is cooked and nicely lacquered, 15 to 20 minutes. Let cool completely, then break each slice into thirds and serve with cocktails.

MAKES ABOUT 50 CANAPÉS

BACON BUZZ
In China, bacon is the primary ingredient in the turnip cake (*law bock gow*) traditionally prepared on New Year's Day to bring good luck and prosperity.

bacon-banana treats

As anybody knows who's ever had a bacon and banana sandwich, the two ingredients couldn't complement one another more. Marinate rounds of banana in a little lemon juice and grainy mustard, wrap them with mellow hickory- or applewood-smoked bacon slices, run them under the broiler, and you have one of the most unusual canapés imaginable. I've also learned that this recipe works equally well with small chunks of fresh (not canned) pineapple.

2 tablespoons lemon juice
1 tablespoon grainy dark mustard
Salt and freshly ground black pepper to taste
2 ripe but firm bananas
8 slices hickory- or applewood-smoked bacon, cut in half

• In a medium bowl, whisk together the lemon juice, mustard, and salt and pepper till thickened. Cut each banana crosswise into 8 rounds, add the rounds to the marinade, stir gently to coat, and let stand about 15 minutes.

• Meanwhile, fry the bacon in a large skillet over moderate heat till half-cooked and drain on paper towels.

• Preheat the oven broiler.

• Wrap each banana round with a piece of bacon, secure each with a toothpick soaked in water, place on the rack of a broiler pan, and broil about 4 inches from the heat till the bacon is crisp, 5 to 6 minutes, turning once. Serve hot or at room temperature.

MAKES 16 CANAPÉS

bacon, cream cheese, and horseradish dip

This is a classic American dip that is ideal for cocktail parties, receptions, picnics, or to keep in the fridge to spread cold on crackers for the occasional snack. I do like the added flavor of hickory in my dip, but nobody will object if you use ordinary cured bacon. Note that the fresh chives add a good deal to the flavor of this dip.

6 thick slices lean hickory-smoked bacon
Two 8-ounce packages cream cheese, at room temperature
1 cup half-and-half
2 tablespoons minced fresh chives
2 tablespoons prepared horseradish
1 teaspoon fresh lemon juice
1 teaspoon Worcestershire sauce
Salt and freshly ground black pepper to taste
Assorted crackers

• In a large skillet, fry the bacon over moderate heat till crisp, drain on paper towels, and crumble finely.

• In a bowl, blend the cream cheese and half-and-half till smooth, add the bacon and remaining ingredients except crackers, and mix till well blended. Cover the dip and let stand about 1 hour before serving with crackers.

MAKES ABOUT 3 CUPS

hot bacon–blue cheese dip

Since the bacon and blue cheese in a classic Cobb salad are the two ingredients that distinguish the Cobb from all other salads, why not, I figured, combine the two to make an unusual dip? Virtually any style of bacon will work for this dip, but what I really love to use is a fine corncob-smoked Vermont bacon. And if you really want the ultimate dip, spring for genuine French Roquefort cheese or a superior domestic blue like Maytag.

6 slices lean smoked bacon
1 small onion, minced
2 tablespoons all-purpose flour
½ cup whole milk
½ cup lager beer
1 teaspoon Worcestershire sauce
Cayenne pepper to taste
½ pound blue cheese, crumbled
Bread sticks

- In a large skillet, fry the bacon over moderate heat till crisp, drain on paper towels, and crumble.
- Pour off all but about 2 tablespoons of fat from the skillet, add the onion, and stir 3 minutes. Add the flour and stir 3 minutes longer. Whisking, add the milk and beer, then add the Worcestershire and cayenne. Bring the mixture to a low boil, whisking, cook for 2 minutes, and remove from the heat. Add the bacon and blue cheese and stir till the cheese is melted.
- Transfer the dip to a small bowl and serve with bread sticks.

MAKES ABOUT 1¾ CUPS

bacon-almond cheese spread

I like this smooth spread with a mellow honey-cured or maple-smoked bacon that seems so compatible with creamy cottage cheese and toasted almonds. I've also made it with more assertive grated extra-sharp Vermont or Canadian cheddar and toasted almonds, in which case a fine double-smoked bacon (like German *Speck* or domestic hickory) is more in order.

5 slices honey-cured or maple-smoked bacon
2 cups creamed cottage cheese
3 tablespoons chopped fresh chives
1 teaspoon Worcestershire sauce
Salt and freshly ground black pepper to taste
¼ cup finely chopped toasted almonds
Toast triangles

• In a large skillet, fry the bacon over moderate heat till crisp, drain on paper towels, and crumble.

• In a blender or food processor, combine the cottage cheese, chives, Worcestershire, and salt and pepper, blend till just smooth, and scrape into a bowl. Add the bacon and almonds, stir till well blended, cover, and chill about 30 minutes before serving on toast triangles.

MAKES ABOUT 2½ CUPS

BACON BONUS
Bacon fried in its own fat cooks crisper than broiled or baked bacon cooked on a slotted drip pan.

bacon-cheddar popcorn

For ages, bacon has had an affinity with corn and cornmeal in any number of traditional American dishes (succotash, johnnycakes, corn chowder, crackling cornbread), so why shouldn't it, along with tangy cheddar cheese, be used to give popcorn a whole new character? What's essential here for optimal flavor is that the bacon fat be added to the cooking oil. To keep the popcorn from losing all crispiness, place it in the oven just till the melted cheese coats the popped kernels the way butter normally would.

4 slices cured bacon
1 tablespoon vegetable oil
½ cup popcorn kernels
¼ pound extra-sharp cheddar cheese, finely grated
Salt to taste

• Preheat the oven to 250°F.

• In a skillet, fry the bacon over moderate heat till crisp, drain on paper towels, and crumble finely.

• Pour 3 tablespoons of the bacon fat into a stove-top popcorn popper or deep, heavy saucepan with a lid, add the oil, and heat over moderately high heat till the mixture begins to smoke. Add the popcorn, cover, and shake the pan till the popping stops. Pour the popcorn into a large ovenproof pot, add the cheese, bacon, and salt, and toss. Heat in the oven till the cheese is melted, about 5 minutes. Serve hot.

bacon-stuffed cremini mushrooms

Wild cremini mushrooms (now available in most supermarkets) may look like cultivated white agarics (buttons), but once you've tasted their earthy, woodsy flavor,
you'll see why they're preferable to the blander variety and are ideal for stuffing.
Although you can also stuff other delicious exotic mushrooms, such as cup-shaped
golden chanterelles, expensive shiitakes, and small portabellas, most of these
require not only a little precooking to ensure tenderness but also extra labor scoop-
ing out cavities in the caps large enough to stuff. Virtually any lean smoked or
unsmoked bacon can be used in the stuffing, but I think the meatiness of Irish or
English bacon (or even fine Canadian bacon) contributes a great deal to the overall
texture.

18 to 20 fresh cremini mushrooms
8 slices Irish or English back bacon, finely chopped
2 tablespoons butter
3 scallions (parts of green leaves included), minced
½ small red bell pepper, seeded and minced
1 garlic clove, minced
1 cup sour cream
¼ teaspoon Worcestershire sauce
¼ teaspoon salt
Freshly ground black pepper to taste

• Wipe the mushrooms clean with a damp cloth, remove the stems and chop them finely, then
arrange the caps open side up in a large, shallow baking dish.

• In a large skillet, fry the bacon over moderate heat till browned and drain on paper towels. Pour all
but 1 tablespoon of grease from the skillet, add the butter, and let melt. Add the chopped mushroom
stems, scallions, bell pepper, and garlic, stir till softened, about 5 minutes, and transfer to a mixing
bowl. Add the bacon pieces, sour cream, Worcestershire, salt, and pepper and mix till well blended.

• Preheat the oven to 350°F.

• Stuff the mushroom cavities with equal amounts of the mixture and bake till the tops are golden,
about 20 minutes. Serve hot as an appetizer.

MAKES ABOUT 6 SERVINGS

clams casino

Legend has it that this classic American appetizer was created around 1917 in The Casino at Narragansett, New York, by a maître d'hôtel for a society lady who requested something really special for her dinner guests. Insisting that the delectable dish be given an identity, she simply named it after the restaurant. Since those gilded days, the dish has traveled to every corner of the country and undergone numerous transformations—in New Orleans, oysters are usually substituted for the clams and served on rock salt—but no matter how the dish is prepared, bacon remains the major key to its success. Artisanal applewood-smoked bacon also makes a sensuous Clams Casino.

4 tablespoons (½ stick) butter
¼ cup minced red bell pepper
2 tablespoons minced chives
1 tablespoon minced parsley leaves
Juice of ½ lemon
½ teaspoon Worcestershire sauce
Salt and freshly ground black pepper to taste
½ cup dry white wine
24 littleneck clams in the shells
3 thick strips hickory-smoked bacon, each cut into 8 pieces
2 tablespoons bread crumbs

• Preheat the oven to 475°F.

• In a small saucepan, melt the butter over moderately low heat, add the bell pepper, chives, parsley, lemon juice, Worcestershire, and salt and pepper, stir about 2 minutes, and remove from the heat.

• In a large skillet, heat the wine over moderately high heat, add the clams, and reduce the heat to moderate. Cover the pan tightly and let the clams steam till they open, about 5 minutes. Remove pan from the heat and carefully pick out and discard the top shell of each clam, retaining the liquor surrounding the clams. (Discard any clams that do not open.)

• Carefully transfer the clams to a large, shallow baking pan, spoon equal amounts of butter sauce over each, top each with a piece of bacon, and sprinkle bread crumbs over the tops. Bake the clams for 5 minutes, increase the oven heat to broil, and broil till the bacon is crispy, 2 to 3 minutes. Serve immediately.

MAKES 4 SERVINGS

bacon-wrapped dungeness crab legs

This was an appetizer I shared with James Beard on more than one occasion on the West Coast, and simple as it is, I still believe it's one of the most delectable dishes ever conceived. The key to its success, of course, is the quality of the two ingredients—and not overcooking the delicate, pinkish white crabmeat. Today, fortunately, fresh Pacific Dungeness crab legs cooked in the shell are available in fine seafood markets across the country during the winter months, and now that so much dry-cured, delicately smoked artisanal bacon is available by mail order and in some markets, there's really no excuse for not preparing this dish correctly.

8 strips dry-cured, smoked bacon (preferably applewood- or maple-smoked)
8 fresh, cooked Dungeness crab legs

- In a large skillet, fry the bacon over moderate heat till half-cooked and drain on paper towels.
- Preheat the oven to 425°F.
- With a nutcracker, crack the crab legs and extract the meat in single, whole pieces. Wrap each piece of meat with a slice of bacon, secure with toothpicks soaked in water or small metal skewers, place the pieces on the rack of a broiler pan, and bake till the bacon is crisp but the crabmeat is not overcooked, about 8 minutes. Serve hot as an appetizer.

MAKES 4 SERVINGS

BACON BANTER
"Hogs are in the highest perfection from two and a half to four years old, and make the best bacon when they do not weigh more than one hundred and fifty or sixty at farthest."
—MARY RANDOLPH, *THE VIRGINIA HOUSE-WIFE*, 1824

french cheese and bacon puffs

Having originated most likely in Burgundy, *gougères* are one of the most delectable of all French delicacies and are served everywhere both as a canapé with wine and, in small ramekins, as an appetizer to a meal. In Paris and throughout most of the northern provinces, the puffs are usually made only with Gruyère cheese, but in the mountainous central and eastern regions, where the pig is king, it's not unusual to find them studded with *lardons* made from smoked or unsmoked slab bacon. There are dozens of different ways to make these puffs, but I find that no technique is easier than simply dropping the batter by tablespoons onto a baking sheet, then letting the puffs crisp in the oven after they've baked. For the right texture, do not use a food processor to make this batter, and if you want to lighten your *gougères* (and enhance their flavor even more), use equal amounts of shredded Gruyère and grated Parmesan cheese.

1 cup water
8 tablespoons (1 stick) butter, cut into pieces
¼ teaspoon salt
1 cup all-purpose flour
4 large eggs
½ pound slab bacon, rind removed, finely diced
1 cup shredded Gruyère cheese

• In a heavy saucepan, combine the water, butter, and salt and bring to a boil. Reduce the heat to low, add the flour, and beat with a wooden spoon till a ball of dough forms. Transfer the dough to a mixing bowl and add the eggs one at a time, beating with an electric mixer on high speed till the batter is just thick enough to hold soft peaks. Transfer the batter to a bowl, cover with plastic wrap, and chill briefly.

• In a large skillet, fry the bacon dice over moderate heat till crisp and drain on paper towels.

• Preheat the oven to 375°F. Butter a large baking sheet.

• Fold the cheese and bacon into the prepared batter till well blended, then drop by tablespoons onto the prepared baking sheet. Bake the puffs 30 minutes, turn off the heat, and let stand till they are golden and crisp, about 10 minutes. Serve the puffs warm.

MAKES ABOUT 36 PUFFS

devils on horseback

In Victorian England, Angels on Horseback were fresh oysters wrapped in streaky bacon, baked, broiled, or grilled till crisp, and served on buttered toast as either an appetizer or a savoury at the end of a meal. Devils on Horseback, by contrast, were marinated prunes stuffed with spicy chutney, wrapped in bacon, smeared with hot mustard, and served in the same manner. Today, only a few traditional London restaurants still offer Angels or Devils (I've had them at both Maggie Jones's and Green's), but at many formal receptions and in no-nonsense country restaurants, these unusual and sapid delicacies are as popular as a century ago. If, by the way, you don't have a really good chutney on hand, it's perfectly permissible to stuff the prunes with whole blanched almonds instead.

16 large prunes, pitted
1 cup dry red wine
2 ounces chutney
16 slices lean streaky bacon
Colman's prepared English mustard
8 toast rounds or rectangles
Soft butter for spreading

• In a bowl, combine the prunes and wine and let soak at least 4 hours.
• Preheat the oven broiler.
• Drain the prunes and stuff each with equal amounts of the chutney, Wrap each prune with a slice of bacon, secure with heavy toothpicks soaked in water, and brush each lightly with mustard. Arrange the prunes on a slotted baking pan and broil about 5 inches from the heat till the bacon is crispy, about 10 minutes, turning once. Drain briefly on paper towels.
• Lightly butter each toast round, arrange 2 Devils on each round, and serve immediately.

MAKES 4 TO 8 SERVINGS

grilled bacon-wrapped date tapas

In Spain, the bacon known as *tocino* is very flavorful cured pig belly that is smoked or unsmoked, and one of its most popular uses (especially in Andalusia) is as a wrapping for all types of tapas found in bars and taverns. You find that everything from local olives to tiny shrimp to veal kidneys are wrapped in bacon and quickly broiled or fried, but one of the most luscious tapas I ever tasted in Seville were dates stuffed with the region's superior almonds, wrapped in lightly smoked *tocino,* and grilled just till the bacon began to crisp. There the tapas were served hot, but they're equally delicious at room temperature. Since neither genuine Spanish *tocino* nor Portuguese *toucinho* is yet available in our markets, use lean streaky bacon (preferably artisanal) for these tapas.

16 pitted dates
16 whole blanched almonds
6 slices streaky bacon, cut crosswise into thirds

- Preheat the oven broiler and position the rack about 4 inches from the heat.
- Stuff each date with an almond, wrap each with a bacon piece, and place seam side down on a slotted broiler pan. Broil till crispy on one side, about 5 minutes, turn, broil till crispy on the other side, and drain on paper towels. Serve hot.

MAKES 16 TAPAS

french country pâté

In France, it is virtually inconceivable to make a classic country pâté without lining the terrine with slices of *lard fumé,* and most serious chefs also add some form of bacon to the basic meat mixture for both flavor and texture. Although you can use a baking dish to make the pâté, nothing distributes the heat more evenly and produces a better texture than an earthenware terrine. Also, if you prefer a fine-textured loaf over a coarse one, use foil to cover the terrine tightly and weight the loaf with a brick or other heavy object while baking. Serve this with rounds of toasted French bread, Dijon mustard, and tiny French *cornichons* (or gherkins).

1½ pounds boneless pork shoulder, trimmed of excess fat
½ pound pork liver
½ pound slab bacon, rind removed
2 scallions (white parts only), finely chopped
2 tablespoons fresh chopped parsley leaves
1 garlic clove, finely chopped
1 tablespoon salt
1 teaspoon freshly ground black pepper
Pinch of allspice
3 large eggs, beaten
1 tablespoon brandy
½ pound thinly sliced streaky bacon (preferably French *lard fumé*)

• Preheat the oven to 350°F.

• Cut the pork shoulder, pork liver, and slab bacon into chunks, place in a food processor, and process till the consistency of well-ground hamburger. Scrape the mixture into a large bowl, add the scallions, parsley, garlic, salt, pepper, allspice, eggs, and brandy, and mix with your hands till thoroughly blended and smooth.

• Line the bottom and sides of a 1½-quart earthenware terrine or baking dish with ¾ of the bacon slices, fill the terrine with the meat mixture, and distribute the mixture evenly with a rubber spatula or large spoon. Top with the remaining bacon slices, cover tightly with a lid or piece of heavy-duty foil, and bake till a knife inserted into the center reveals no red juices, 1½ to 1¾ hours.

• Let the pâté cool completely, then chill at least 2 hours before serving in slices.

MAKES ABOUT 8 APPETIZER SERVINGS

japanese bacon tempura

In the traditional Japanese kitchen, tempura intended to be served as an appetizer or side dish is almost always made with either seafood or vegetables. Innovative chefs today, however, are devising ways to use various meats for tempura, and one of the most popular is the pungent, double-smoked commercial and artisanal bacon now available in more and more markets. When carefully battered and fried till crisp and puffy, it's a veritable sensation, either by itself or dipped into a Japanese soy sauce sweetened with sake.

12 thick-cut slices double-smoked bacon
1 large egg
1 cup ice water
1¼ cups all-purpose flour
Sesame or vegetable oil
Salt to taste

- In a large skillet, fry half the bacon slices over moderate heat till browned but not crisp, about 10 minutes, turning once. Drain on paper towels and repeat with remaining slices.
- In a bowl, whisk together the egg and ice water, then gradually whisk in the flour till the batter is smooth.
- Pour about 2 inches of oil in a wok or heavy medium saucepan and heat over moderate heat till the temperature registers 375°F on a deep-fat thermometer.
- Working in batches, dip the bacon slices into the batter and deep-fry them till crisp and puffy, 5 to 7 minutes. Drain on a wire rack, season with salt, and serve immediately as a canapé (each piece broken in half) or an appetizer.

MAKES 4 TO 6 APPETIZER SERVINGS

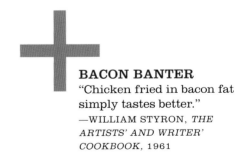

BACON BANTER
"Chicken fried in bacon fat simply tastes better."
—WILLIAM STYRON, *THE ARTISTS' AND WRITER' COOKBOOK,* 1961

pancetta and mozzarella pizzas

Probably the most memorable pizzas I've ever eaten were small ones made with tangy *mozzarella di bufala* (water buffalo mozzarella) and *guanciale* bacon at a trattoria in Salerno, Italy, south of Naples. Unfortunately, most of the imported *bufala* mozzarella sold in some of our markets is a far cry from the utterly fresh product found in Italy, so the next best thing is the superb cow's milk mozzarella made by Italian grocers all over the country. (For pizza, you want the dry cheese, not the balls floating in water, which are too moist.) *Guanciale* is bacon cut from the jowl and cheek of hogs, cured with flavorings, and lightly smoked. You might find it in Italian markets, but a well-cured pancetta is just as good for these pizzas. Cut into wedges, the pizzas also make clever canapés to pass at cocktail parties.

THE PIZZA DOUGH
1 envelope active dry yeast
1 cup lukewarm water
4 cups all-purpose flour
1 teaspoon salt
2 tablespoons olive oil

THE TOPPING
¼ cup olive oil
2 tablespoons chopped fresh basil
1½ pounds fresh dry mozzarella cheese, grated
10 plum tomatoes, sliced
2 garlic cloves, minced
2 red bell peppers, minced and sautéed 2 minutes in 2 tablespoons olive oil
½ pound pancetta, diced
1 large red onion, minced

• To make the dough, sprinkle the yeast over the water in a small bowl, stir, and let proof till bubbly, about 10 minutes.

• In a large bowl, combine 3¾ cups of the flour and the salt, add the yeast mixture plus the olive oil, and mix till a firm ball of dough can be formed. Sprinkle the remaining ¼ cup flour on a work surface, place ball of dough on the flour, and knead till the dough is elastic, about 10 minutes. Place the dough in a greased bowl, turn to coat the sides evenly, cover with a towel, and let rise in a warm area till doubled in bulk, at least 1 hour.

• Preheat the oven to 400°F.

(continued)

• Punch the dough down and divide into 6 equal parts. On a lightly floured surface, roll out or stretch the parts into six 6-inch circles and fit on individual pizza pans or heavy-gauge baking sheets. Brush the tops with olive oil and sprinkle each with basil. Sprinkle equal amounts of cheese over each circle and top with equal amounts of tomatoes, garlic, sautéed peppers, pancetta, and onion. Bake in the upper third of the oven till the crusts are golden brown, about 15 minutes, and serve as soon as possible.

MAKES 6 SMALL PIZZAS

BACON BUZZ
In Italy, at least half a dozen distinctive styles of pancetta are used to enhance multiple meat, poultry, and pasta preparations.

breakfast
and brunch
dishes

Quiche Lorraine

Alsatian Bacon and Onion Tart

Bacon, Goat Cheese, and Vidalia Onion Pie

English Bacon and Egg Pie

Danish Potato, Tomato, and Bacon Omelette

Scandinavian Bacon and Egg Cake

Southern Corn and Bacon Soufflé

French Cheese and Bacon Soufflé

Italian Open-Faced Zucchini and Bacon Omelette

New England Apple and Bacon Griddlecakes

Venezuelan Squash, Potato, and Bacon Pancakes

French Toast and Canadian Bacon Breakfast Sandwiches

Bacon Toad-in-the-Hole

Bacon Scrapple

California Hangtown Fry

Russian Hash and Eggs

Skewered Fried Smelts and Bacon

Twice-Cooked Chinese Bacon

quiche lorraine

Originally made with a bread dough crust and cooked in a baker's oven, quiche was traditionally served after a regional dish of suckling pig in aspic on May Day in the French province of Lorraine. Today, quiche lorraine is probably France's most famous bacon preparation in all its many guises, and I must say that there's still really nothing more delectable for brunch than a golden, cus-tardy quiche studded with premium bacon and served with a good salad and plenty of Beaujolais. I admit I'm as guilty as the next cook when I sometimes add a little grated Gruyère cheese, diced onions, or herbs to my quiche, but when I'm determined to make the dish as authentic as possible, I do go out of my way to acquire real French smoked bacon (*lard fumé*) or beautifully cured rolled pork breast (*ventrèche*). Otherwise, I use fairly lean slab bacon. Do note that any quiche lorraine should be served warm, not hot, after it's had a while to set prop-erly. This quiche is even good cold.

THE PASTRY
1¾ cups all-purpose flour
12 tablespoons (1½ sticks) butter
1 teaspoon salt
2 to 3 tablespoons ice water

THE FILLING
1 tablespoon butter
½ pound slab bacon, rind removed, diced
1½ cups heavy cream
3 large eggs
Salt and freshly ground black pepper to taste
Pinch of grated nutmeg

• Lightly butter a 9- to 10-inch tart pan or pie plate and set aside.

• To make the pastry, combine the flour and butter in a mixing bowl and rub with your fingertips till particles the size of peas form. Add 2 tablespoons of the water and, using your fingertips, mix as quickly and lightly as possible till the dough is smooth, adding more water as needed. (Do not knead.) Wrap the dough in plastic wrap and chill till firm, 20 to 30 minutes.

• Preheat the oven to 375°F.

• On a lightly floured surface, roll out the dough wide enough to fit the prepared tart pan and press it onto the bottom and sides of the pan. Prick the dough all over with a fork, crimp the edges, and bake till golden, about 20 minutes. Let the pastry shell cool on a wire rack.

• For the filling, melt the butter in a large skillet over moderate heat, add the bacon, and stir till browned, about 7 minutes. Drain on paper towels, then sprinkle evenly over the bottom of the pastry shell. In a bowl, whisk together the cream, eggs, salt and pepper, and nutmeg till well blended, pour the mixture over the bacon, and bake till the filling is set and the quiche is puffy and golden brown, 30 to 35 minutes. Serve warm.

MAKES 4 TO 6 SERVINGS

BACON BUZZ
Although the Old French term for pork was *bako,* today the French word for bacon is *lard,* magnifying the linguistic confusion in English over the rendered bacon cooking fat by the same name.

alsatian bacon and onion tart

Also called *tarte à la flamme* in French, this delectable Alsatian tart was originally made in a baker's wood-fired oven and traditionally eaten by workers in the morning with a glass or two of spicy Gewürztraminer wine. (Today in Alsace, the tart is popular virtually at any time of day, for any occasion, and I think it's a perfect treat for brunch.) Ideally, the tart should be made with fresh pot cheese, found occasionally in our finest food shops, but if that's unavailable, low-fat ricotta works beautifully (as do equal parts of whipped cream cheese and crème fraîche). And since both French *ventrèche* bacon (cured and smoked pig breast) and German Black Forest bacon can now be found either in some upscale butcher shops and delis or online, do try to use what the Alsatians use. Otherwise, choose top-quality slab bacon, with the rind removed and the meat and fat cut into medium slices.

THE PASTRY
1¾ cups all-purpose flour
8 tablespoons (1 stick) chilled butter, cut into pieces
1 teaspoon salt
2 tablespoons ice water

THE FILLING
6 to 8 slices *ventrèche* or Black Forest bacon
½ cup farmer's pot cheese (or low-fat ricotta, beaten)
½ cup half-and-half
1 tablespoon all-purpose flour
1 teaspoon salt
2 tablespoons vegetable oil
1 large onion, thinly sliced

• To make the pastry, sift the flour onto a work surface, place the butter in the center, and rub with your fingertips till tiny particles are formed. Make a well in the mixture, add the salt and water, and mix quickly with your fingertips till the dough is smooth. Form the dough into a ball, wrap in plastic wrap, and chill about 30 minutes.

• Preheat the oven to 400°F. Butter a heavy baking sheet and set aside.

• To make the filling, fry the bacon in a large skillet over moderate heat till almost crisp, drain on paper towels, and chop coarsely. Set aside.

• Roll out the dough to form a thin rectangle about 7 by 10 inches, place on the prepared baking sheet, and form a slight border by pinching the edges upward. In a bowl, combine the cheese, half-and-half, flour, salt, and oil, mix till well blended, and spoon the mixture evenly over the bottom of the pastry shell. Distribute the onion slices over the top, sprinkle on the bacon, and bake for 15 to 20 minutes or till the pastry is golden brown. Cut the tart into rectangles to serve.

MAKES 4 TO 6 SERVINGS

BACON BUZZ
Up till the eighteenth century, *bacon* was a general term for all forms of pork in many European countries.

bacon, goat cheese, and vidalia onion pie

This rich pie is not only a symphony of contrasting flavors and textures but also the perfect dish to serve at a stylish brunch. Peppered slab bacon is now available both online and in many better supermarkets, and while you could simply chop the bacon and include it with the sweet onions in the filling, draping it over the top makes a much more impressive presentation and highlights the distinctive bacon. Notice that this pie needs no salt. I serve the pie with only a vinegary green salad (preferably arugula during the summer) or a platter of fresh fruit.

THE PASTRY
1½ cups all-purpose flour
12 tablespoons vegetable shortening, chilled
1 teaspoon salt
3 to 4 tablespoons ice water

THE FILLING
2 tablespoons butter
2 medium Vidalia onions, thinly sliced
¾ cup crumbled goat cheese
½ cup half-and-half
4 ounces peppered slab bacon, rind removed, cut into ⅛-inch-thick slices

• To make the pastry, place the flour, shortening, and salt in a food processor and pulse till the mixture resembles coarse meal. Using short pulses, gradually add enough water to form a dough that holds together but does not form a ball. Wrap the dough in plastic wrap and chill for 1 hour.

• Preheat the oven to 400°F.

• On a lightly floured surface, roll out the dough to fit a 9-inch pie plate, line the plate with the dough, and crimp the edges. Prick the dough all over with a fork, bake till just golden, about 20 minutes, and let cool on a wire rack.

• Reduce the oven temperature to 350°F.

• To make the filling, melt the butter in a large skillet over moderate heat, add the onions, and stir till softened and translucent. Pile the onions evenly in the prepared pie shell, sprinkle the cheese evenly over the top, and pour the half-and-half over the cheese. Arrange the bacon slices over the top, overlapping them slightly if necessary, and bake till the bacon is crisp, 45 to 50 minutes. Let cool slightly, then serve in wedges.

MAKES 4 SERVINGS

english bacon and egg pie

The savoury pie has been an English art for centuries, and while many of the "raised" ones are pretty complicated affairs, this simple bacon and egg pie is the type a housewife prepares with great ease for a casual weekend midday meal and serves with something like a watercress and endive salad and glasses of pale ale. (Since the pie is almost as good cold as warm, it's also a favorite for picnics.) For the crust to be properly light and crispy, be sure to use nothing but lard to make the dough, and if the bacon doesn't have much fat on the ends, fry it in a little butter.

THE PASTRY
2 cups all-purpose flour
$\frac{2}{3}$ cup lard, chilled and cut up
1 teaspoon salt
4 to 6 tablespoons ice water

THE FILLING
5 large eggs
6 slices English or Irish bacon, cut into $\frac{1}{2}$-inch pieces
1 cup half-and-half
Salt and freshly ground black pepper to taste
Milk for brushing

• To make the pastry, combine the flour, lard, and salt in a mixing bowl and work with your fingertips till the mixture is mealy. Add 2 to 3 tablespoons of the water, mix till the pastry holds together, then continue adding just enough water to make a smooth ball of dough. Wrap in plastic wrap and chill about 20 minutes.

• Meanwhile, place 3 of the eggs in a saucepan with enough water to cover, bring to a boil, reduce the heat to moderate, and hard-boil the eggs for 9 minutes. Drain, cool the eggs under cold running water, then peel and chop them coarsely.

• Preheat the oven to 400°F. Grease a 9-inch pie plate and set aside.

• In a large skillet, fry the bacon over moderately low heat till lightly browned, about 5 minutes, and drain on paper towels.

• Divide the chilled pastry in half on a floured surface, roll out one half wide enough to line the bottom and sides of the prepared pie plate, and scatter the chopped eggs and bacon evenly over the bottom. Beat the 2 remaining eggs with the half-and-half and salt and pepper till well blended and pour over the pie. Roll out the remaining dough wide enough to cover the pie, dampen the edges with a little water, and press the edges to seal. Cut a small vent in the center of the pastry lid, brush the lid with milk, and bake in the upper third of the oven for 10 minutes. Reduce the heat to 350°F and continue baking till golden brown, about 30 minutes. Let the pie stand about 10 minutes before serving.

MAKES 4 SERVINGS

danish potato, tomato, and bacon omelette

In Denmark, this popular breakfast omelette (*aegkage*) is made with the superior lean bacon made from specially bred Landrace pigs. Normally, a good substitute would be English or Canadian bacon, if the Danish product is unavailable, but since neither really renders enough fat to fully flavor the other ingredients, the best option is a nice chunk of domestic slab bacon—found in most supermarkets— or even ordinary sliced bacon. For a brunch variation, this omelette could also be made with chopped broccoli, asparagus, zucchini, and/or grated sharp cheese, so feel free to experiment. Do note that since Danish bacon tends to be salty, no salt is needed—especially if you add any well-aged cheese.

½ pound sliced Danish bacon (or lean slab bacon, rind removed), cut into 1-inch pieces
1 medium potato, shredded
1 small onion, finely chopped
1 small ripe tomato, seeded and finely chopped
6 large eggs
½ cup whole milk
1 tablespoon minced chives
Freshly ground black pepper to taste

- Preheat the oven to 350°F.
- In a large skillet, fry the bacon over moderate heat till almost crisp and drain on paper towels. Pour off all but about 1 tablespoon of the fat, add the potato, onion, and tomato, and stir till the potato is softened, about 5 minutes.
- In a bowl, whisk together the eggs and milk, pour over the vegetables, and stir slightly. Add the bacon, chives, and pepper, stir, and bake in the oven till the omelette is set, 20 to 25 minutes. Cut into wedges and serve hot.

MAKES 3 TO 4 SERVINGS

BACON BUZZ
Today, the finest Danish bacon is still produced from Landrace pigs, a breed developed in the nineteenth century.

scandinavian bacon and egg cake

Breakfast is as important a meal throughout Scandinavia as it is in Britain and the American South, and since pork is the major meat there, lean back bacon produced from specially bred pigs is used to make numerous hearty dishes. Traditionally, in Denmark and Norway, this custardy cake (*flaeskeaeggekage*) is always prepared on top of the stove, and since cooks are so proud of their superior smoked bacon, they almost always highlight it by simply arranging the slices around the edges of the cake and serving everything directly from the skillet. In recent years, exports of genuine Danish bacon to the United States have increased steadily, so look for it in the better markets. Do be aware, however, that this bacon can be very salty, meaning that should you decide to incorporate it in the egg mixture instead of serving it separately (as I've done with great success), no salt should be added. (Some people might even prefer to soak the bacon about an hour in fresh water to remove some of the salt.) To prevent the bottom of this cake from burning, I strongly suggest you use a heavy enameled skillet and maintain the heat at very low.

½ **pound sliced Danish bacon (or sliced hickory-smoked bacon), cut in half crosswise**
6 large eggs
1 tablespoon all-purpose flour
Freshly ground black pepper to taste
½ **cup half-and-half**
3 tablespoons finely chopped fresh dill

• In a large, heavy skillet, fry the bacon till almost crisp, drain on paper towels, and keep warm on a plate in a low oven. Pour all but about 1 tablespoon of fat from the skillet.

• In a mixing bowl, whisk together the eggs, flour, and pepper till just blended, then slowly add the half-and-half, whisking till the ingredients are well blended and frothy. Warm the fat in the skillet over moderate heat and add the egg mixture. Reduce the heat to very low and, without stirring, let the mixture set into a firm custard, about 20 minutes, watching to make sure the bottom of the cake doesn't burn.

• To serve from the skillet, arrange the bacon slices around the edges of the cake, sprinkle the dill over the top, and cut into wedges.

MAKES 4 SERVINGS

southern corn and bacon soufflé

In the American South (unlike in France), *soufflé* refers simply to any composed baked vegetable dish that contains eggs, and none is more elegant than this corn and bacon soufflé enhanced by either sharp cheddar or freshly grated Parmesan cheese. The soufflé could be served as a vegetable side dish, but I like to feature it at brunch with a large green salad and maybe thin slices of cured country ham. The soufflé should be just golden brown on top and puffy.

½ pound sliced hickory-smoked bacon
6 tablespoons (¾ stick) butter
¼ cup freshly grated Parmesan cheese
1 medium onion, finely chopped
1½ cups whole corn kernels, fresh or frozen and thawed
3 tablespoons all-purpose flour
2 cups milk, heated
6 large eggs
Salt and freshly ground black pepper to taste
Cayenne pepper to taste

• In a large skillet, fry the bacon over moderate heat till crisp, drain on paper towels, and crumble. Pour off all but about 1 tablespoon of fat from the skillet.

• Grease the bottom and sides of a 1½-quart soufflé or baking dish with 1 tablespoon of the butter, coat the surfaces with half the grated cheese, and set aside.

• Add 2 tablespoons of the butter to the skillet and melt over moderate heat. Add the onion and corn, stir for 3 minutes, and set aside.

• Preheat the oven to 375°F.

• In a saucepan, melt the remaining 3 tablespoons of the butter over low heat, add the flour, and whisk till golden, 2 to 3 minutes. Remove pan from the heat, add the milk, and whisk till thickened and smooth. Cool the mixture slightly, then whisk in the eggs one at a time till well blended. Add the corn mixture, bacon, salt and pepper, and cayenne and blend thoroughly. Scrape the mixture into the prepared soufflé dish, sprinkle the remaining cheese over the top, and bake till golden brown, 30 to 35 minutes. Serve hot.

MAKES 4 SERVINGS

french cheese and bacon soufflé

One of the world's greatest cheeses is Comté, produced from Alpine cow's milk in France's eastern Jura region and similar in flavor and texture to Swiss Gruyère. And when you combine Comté with the same area's aromatic *lard fumé* to make this sublime cheese and bacon soufflé, you have a special brunch or luncheon dish worthy of the most sophisticated occasion. Genuine Comté, available in our finest cheese shops, carries a bell symbol and the word *Comté* stamped in green on the rind. If you can't find the cheese, however, use Gruyère. Likewise, *lard fumé* has its own utterly distinctive smoky flavor and aroma, but if it's unavailable, substitute an artisanal double-smoked bacon.

6 slices French *lard fumé* (or double-smoked bacon)
2 tablespoons butter
½ cup finely chopped onion
3 tablespoons all-purpose flour
1½ cups milk
6 ounces Comté (or Gruyère) cheese, grated
Salt and freshly ground black pepper to taste
4 large eggs, separated
Pinch of salt

• In a large skillet, fry the bacon over moderate heat till crisp, drain on paper towels, and crumble. Reserve the bacon fat.

• Preheat the oven to 375°F. Butter a 1½-quart soufflé dish and set aside.

• In a heavy saucepan, combine 2 tablespoons of the bacon fat and butter over moderately low heat, add the onions, and stir till softened, about 2 minutes. Sprinkle the flour over the top and stir about 3 minutes. Gradually add the milk, whisking, increase the heat to high, and boil the mixture for 2 minutes, whisking. Remove the pan from the heat, add the cheese and salt and pepper, and whisk till the cheese is melted. Add the egg yolks one at a time, whisking, then stir in the crumbled bacon.

• In a bowl, beat the egg whites and a pinch of salt with an electric mixer till they hold stiff peaks. Whisk about ¼ of the whites into the cheese mixture, then gently fold in the remaining whites till well blended. Scrape the mixture into the prepared soufflé dish and bake in center of the oven till puffy and golden, 30 to 35 minutes. Serve immediately.

MAKES 4 SERVINGS

italian open-faced zucchini and bacon omelette

Unlike a soft, often runny (*baveuse*) French omelette, an Italian frittata is a firm but never dry open-faced omelette that makes a perfect breakfast or brunch dish. Numerous primary ingredients can be used to make frittatas, but none are as popular as small, tender zucchini and diced pancetta that has just the right proportion of fat and lean meat. What is strategic about this (or any other) frittata is that you use a heavy skillet over moderately low heat to prevent the bottom from over-browning. As in Italy, I like to serve the frittata with a few cold cuts and fresh fruit.

6 ounces pancetta, diced
¼ cup olive oil
1 medium onion, thinly sliced
3 small zucchini, washed and cut into ¼-inch-thick disks
6 large eggs
Salt and freshly ground black pepper to taste
½ cup freshly grated Parmesan cheese
4 tablespoons butter
1 tablespoon finely chopped parsley leaves
3 fresh basil leaves, roughly chopped

• In a large, heavy skillet, cook the pancetta over moderate heat just till lightly browned, about 5 minutes, stirring, and drain on paper towels. Add the olive oil to the skillet, add the onion and zucchini, and stir till the zucchini is lightly browned, about 5 minutes. Drain off the oil and any liquid, transfer the vegetables to a bowl, and let cool.

• Preheat the oven broiler.

• In another large bowl, combine the eggs and salt and pepper and beat till well blended and frothy. Add the onion and zucchini and half the cheese and stir well. In a heavy 10-inch skillet, melt the butter over moderately low heat till it begins to foam, and pour the vegetable mixture into the pan. Add the parsley and basil, reduce the heat to very low, and let cook till the eggs are set but the top is still very moist, about 20 minutes. Sprinkle the remaining ¼ cup cheese over the top and run the skillet under the broiler till the top of the frittata is set but not browned, 30 seconds to 1 minute. Run a sharp knife around the edges to loosen the frittata from the pan, slide it onto a plate, let cool slightly, and serve in wedges.

MAKES 4 SERVINGS

new england apple and bacon griddlecakes

While it might seem logical to use maple-cured or -smoked bacon for this homey recipe, I find that if you use pure maple syrup to pour over the griddlecakes—and the difference between a genuine amber Grade B syrup and the virtually mapleless commercial table syrup product is truly astonishing—the overall maple effect is just too intense. Better to go with a mellow apple-smoked artisanal bacon, which only slightly intensifies the flavor of the apples themselves while adding a subtle smokiness to the batter. There's also nothing wrong with using a mildly peppered bacon for an altogether different effect.

½ pound applewood-smoked bacon
1½ cups all-purpose flour
2 tablespoons sugar
2 teaspoons baking powder
1 teaspoon baking soda
1 teaspoon salt
¼ teaspoon ground cinnamon
2 large eggs
½ cup whole milk
2 Granny Smith apples, peeled and coarsely grated
4 tablespoons (½ stick) butter, melted, plus extra for serving
Pure maple syrup (preferably Grade B)

- In a large skillet, fry the bacon till crisp, drain on paper towels, and crumble.
- In a large bowl, combine the flour, sugar, baking powder, baking soda, salt, and cinnamon and stir till well blended. In another bowl, whisk together the eggs and milk, add to the flour mixture, and stir till the batter is just blended. Stir in the apples and bacon.
- Heat a griddle or large, heavy skillet over moderately high heat till hot and brush it with butter. Drop the batter by ¼-cup measures onto the griddle and cook till bubbles appear on the surface and the edges begin to brown, about 2 minutes. Turn with a spatula and cook till golden, about 1 minute longer. Transfer the griddlecakes to a platter, keep warm in a low oven, and continue to make more griddlecakes in the same manner. Serve hot with butter and maple syrup.

MAKES 4 SERVINGS

venezuelan squash, potato, and bacon pancakes

Native to the Western Hemisphere, squash has been cultivated in South America for at least the past two thousand years, and nowhere is it cooked with keener imagination and expertise than in Venezuela. These breakfast pancakes, for instance, depend not only on plenty of smoky bacon to add flavor to the bland squash but also on bacon grease for cooking the cakes to the right crispness. Any winter squash can be used, but since butternut's orange flesh seems the sweetest to me, I always look for the relatively large, smooth, yellowish gourds. Ordinary hickory-smoked supermarket bacon is just fine for this dish, so long, that is, as it has enough fat to render adequate drippings.

½ pound sliced streaky bacon, cut into ¼-inch pieces
One 2-pound butternut squash, peeled, seeded, and coarsely grated
2 russet potatoes, peeled and coarsely grated
1 medium onion, finely grated
3 large eggs, beaten
Salt and freshly ground black pepper to taste
Sour cream

• In a large, heavy skillet, fry the bacon over moderate heat till almost crisp and drain on paper towels. Strain the bacon fat into a small bowl and reserve.

• In a large bowl, combine the squash, potatoes, onion, eggs, bacon, and salt and pepper and mix with your hands till well blended. In the same skillet, heat about 1 tablespoon of the reserved bacon fat over moderately high heat and tilt the pan back and forth to coat the bottom and sides.

• Spoon enough of the squash mixture into the pan to form a compact 1-inch-thick pancake, spreading it evenly with a spatula to within 1 inch of the sides of the pan. Cook till the bottom is browned and crisp, about 3 minutes, then invert the pancake onto a plate. Add 1 more tablespoon of bacon fat to the skillet, slide the uncooked side of the pancake into the pan, and cook till the bottom is browned and crisp, about 3 minutes.

• Transfer the pancake to a platter, keep warm in a low oven, and continue making pancakes with the remaining bacon fat and mixture in the same manner. Serve hot with dollops of sour cream.

MAKES 6 SERVINGS

french toast and canadian bacon breakfast sandwiches

This is a breakfast recipe I came up with when a friend brought me my first chunk of genuine peameal Canadian bacon—sweet-pickle-cured back bacon coated in corn-meal. Ordinary cylinders of Canadian-style bacon (which is more like ham than bacon) found in all supermarkets are perfectly acceptable for these sandwiches, but once you've tasted the sweeter, moister peameal original (which can easily be ordered online), you'll understand why some American enthusiasts are now plan-ning special trips to Canada just to stock up on this unique bacon. And if you go to the trouble to acquire it, also be sure to use pure maple syrup to drizzle over these sandwiches (Grade A is the lightest, subtlest syrup, but amber Grade B's full flavor and sturdier body make it preferable for most breakfast dishes).

8 tablespoons (1 stick) plus 3 tablespoons butter
Eight to ten ¼-inch-thick slices Canadian bacon (preferably peameal bacon)
12 large eggs
1 cup whole milk
Salt and cayenne pepper to taste
8 to 10 slices white loaf bread, crusts removed
Pure maple syrup (preferably Grade B)

• In a large skillet, melt the 3 tablespoons of butter over moderate heat, add the bacon slices, brown lightly, about 2 minutes on each side, and keep warm on a plate.

• In a shallow bowl, whisk together 6 of the eggs with the milk, salt, and cayenne till well blended. In another bowl, whisk the remaining 6 eggs till frothy.

• Cut each slice of bread in half diagonally. Soak each slice momentarily in the milk mixture, then, using two forks or large spoons, carefully coat both sides of each slice in the beaten egg, placing the slices on a plate as they are coated.

• In a large skillet, heat about ⅓ of the stick of butter over moderate heat, add about ⅓ of the coated slices, cook about 3 minutes on each side till golden, and transfer the toast to a plate with a spatula. Repeat the procedure with the remaining butter and slices.

• Cut the Canadian bacon into approximately the same size triangles as the toast, sandwich one bacon slice between two pieces of toast, arrange the sandwiches on a large heated platter, and drizzle them liberally with maple syrup.

MAKES 4 TO 5 SERVINGS

bacon toad-in-the-hole

Okay, so genuine British toad-in-the-hole usually involves small English breakfast sausages baked inside a batter pastry (like Yorkshire pudding) and served at lunch in modest taverns, restaurants, and even pubs. No doubt it's a humble dish, so you can imagine my surprise when, some years back, I was served this updated and much more elegant version made with eggs, English bacon, and brioche at no other than the swanky Savoy hotel in London. Some would say there's nothing "toad-in-the-hole" about it. I say what's in a name, and that it's simply one of the most sublime breakfast dishes you can serve. If you like, you can retain and toast the cutout bread rounds and serve them on the side of each portion to smear marmalade or fruit preserves on.

6 thick slices brioche
6 tablespoons (¾ stick) butter, melted, plus 3 tablespoons solid
1 dozen large eggs
Salt and freshly ground black pepper to taste
6 ounces English or Irish back bacon (or sliced Canadian bacon), chopped
6 tablespoons sour cream
3 tablespoons minced fresh chives

- Preheat the oven to 425°F.
- Brush both sides of the brioche slices with melted butter, then, using a 2½-inch biscuit cutter, cut out and discard a round from the center of each slice. Arrange the slices on a large baking sheet, toast in the oven on one side till golden brown, 8 to 9 minutes, and keep warm.
- In a large bowl, whisk together the eggs and salt and pepper and set aside.
- In a large, heavy skillet, melt the 3 tablespoons of solid butter over moderate heat, add the bacon, and stir till lightly browned, about 4 minutes. Add the eggs, reduce the heat slightly, and slowly stir till the eggs are set but still almost creamy, about 4 minutes.
- To serve, arrange the toasted brioche slices on 6 individual serving plates, spoon equal amounts of eggs and bacon into the holes, and top each with a tablespoon of sour cream and some of the chives.

MAKES 6 SERVINGS

bacon scrapple

Although scrapple was created by the Pennsylvania Dutch, today the breakfast dish is most closely associated with the city of Philadelphia. Traditionally, scrapple is made with calf's liver, pig's knuckles, and seasonings, bound with cornmeal into a mush, and fried, making it, for some, an acquired taste. This version using bacon was created by my West Coast colleague and friend Marion Cunningham, and much as I personally love the genuine dish with fried eggs and biscuits, I must say the bacon rendition was a revelation—especially when made with either a superior maple-cured bacon or a gutsy double-smoked one. One word of advice: to prevent the cornmeal from becoming lumpy when added to boiling liquid, always stir it first into a little cold water.

$\frac{1}{2}$ **pound maple-cured bacon slices**
1 cup yellow cornmeal
4 cups cold water
1 teaspoon salt
$\frac{1}{2}$ **teaspoon freshly ground black pepper**
1 bay leaf, crumbled

• In a large skillet, fry the bacon till crisp, drain on paper towels, and chop into small pieces. Reserve the bacon fat.

• In a small bowl, stir the cornmeal into 1 cup of the cold water. In a heavy saucepan, bring the remaining 3 cups of water to a boil and add the salt, pepper, and bay leaf. Stir in the cornmeal and 4 tablespoons of the reserved bacon fat, reduce the heat to moderate, and cook, stirring often, till the mixture is thickened, about 20 minutes. Remove pan from the heat and stir in the bacon pieces.

• Grease an $8\frac{1}{2}$-by-$4\frac{1}{2}$-by-$2\frac{1}{2}$-inch loaf pan and scrape the scrapple into the pan. Let cool, cover with plastic wrap, and chill till set and firm, at least 4 hours.

• Cut the loaf into $\frac{1}{2}$-inch slices. In a skillet, heat a little of the bacon fat over moderate heat and fry each slice of scrapple till browned and crisp around the edges, about 5 minutes on each side. Serve hot.

MAKES 4 TO 6 SERVINGS

california hangtown fry

One of America's most original and sensational breakfast or lunch dishes, hangtown fry was supposedly created during the California Gold Rush when, late one morning, a lucky miner came into a restaurant in the rowdy burg of Hangtown (so called because of the town's frequent hangings and today named Placerville) and announced that he wanted the most expensive meal the chef could come up with. Gradually, the dish gained local celebrity and can still be ordered in San Francisco at old-time grills like Tadisch's and Sam's. This is a dish that truly deserves the finest artisanal bacon you can find, and while I personally love the snappy flavor of peppered bacon, feel free to experiment with any style.

8 thick slices peppered bacon
½ cup white cornmeal
Salt and freshly ground black pepper to taste
1 dozen fresh oysters, drained
8 large eggs
3 tablespoons heavy cream
Tabasco sauce to taste
3 tablespoons butter
Chopped parsley leaves, for garnish

• In a large, heavy skillet, fry the bacon slowly over moderately low heat till crisp, drain on paper towels, and crumble. Pour off all but about 1 tablespoon of fat from the skillet and set aside.

• In a small bowl, combine the cornmeal and salt and pepper and mix till well blended. Dip the oysters into the cornmeal, coat lightly, and transfer to a plate. In another bowl, whisk together the eggs, cream, and Tabasco and set aside.

• Add the butter to the fat in the skillet and melt over moderate heat. Add the oysters and cook till they begin to curl, about 1 minute on each side. Add the egg mixture and bacon, reduce the heat to low, and cook till the edges are set, about 2 minutes. Lift the edges with a fork and tilt the pan back and forth so the uncooked egg runs underneath. Continue to cook slowly just till the eggs are set, 3 to 4 minutes. Slide the fry onto a heated platter, garnish the edges with parsley, and serve hot in individual portions.

MAKES 3 TO 4 SERVINGS

russian hash and eggs

A specialty of the Ukraine, this earthy Russian dish (*krestianskiy zavtrak*) is typically served with fried paprika potatoes as a midday meal, and as if the dish were not hearty enough, some home cooks also add a little diced kielbasa or other smoked sausage to the bacon. For brunch, the hash calls for nothing more than a nice selection of fresh fruit (preferably in a compote) and perhaps a pitcher of chilled apple cider.

8 tablespoons (1 stick) butter
2 cups ½-inch-diced day-old pumpernickel bread
½ pound lean double-smoked bacon slices, cut into small pieces
1 medium onion, chopped
Salt and freshly ground black pepper to taste
8 large eggs
Finely chopped fresh dill, for garnish

• In a large skillet, melt half the butter over moderate heat, add the bread, and cook, stirring, till golden brown and crispy, about 8 minutes. Transfer the bread to a large bowl and set aside.

• Add the bacon to the skillet and fry over moderate heat till half-cooked. Add the onion and continue cooking, stirring, till the bacon is crisp and the onion golden, about 5 minutes. Add the bacon, onion, and salt and pepper to the bread, mix till well blended, and keep the hash warm in a low oven. Discard any grease from the skillet and wipe the skillet with paper towels.

• In the skillet, melt 1 tablespoon of the remaining butter, break 2 of the eggs into the skillet, cover, and fry the eggs just till the whites are set and the yolks slightly steamed and still soft, about 1 minute. Transfer the eggs to a warm platter and keep warm in the oven while frying the remaining eggs in the remaining butter.

• To serve, spoon a mound of hash in the center of each of 4 serving plates, press the mounds down with a metal spatula, and top each mound with two of the fried eggs. Sprinkle dill over the tops.

MAKES 4 SERVINGS

BACON BONUS
To prevent long slices of streaky bacon from over-extending the sides of a skillet and not frying evenly, first cut the raw bacon in half crosswise.

skewered fried smelts and bacon

Native to North America, small silvery smelts (also called whitebait), measuring four to five inches in length, are one of the most delectable and neglected fish on today's market. They have a delicate flesh that is rich and oily, and when skewered with a fragrant bacon and quickly deep-fried, they make an unusual brunch dish. Since fresh smelts are very perishable, they are generally flash-frozen shortly after being netted and are marketed whole—to be eaten heads, bones, viscera, and all. (I have little use for the canned smelts, which tend to be too salty and almost mushy.) Larger smelts can also simply be wrapped in bacon, secured with tiny metal skewers or toothpicks soaked in water, and deep-fried till the bacon begins to crisp.

½ pound applewood- or corncob-smoked bacon slices
2 large eggs
½ cup whole milk
Tabasco sauce to taste
1 to 1½ cups all-purpose flour
Dry bread crumbs, for rolling
12 to 15 smelts (about 1½ pounds)
Vegetable oil, for frying

- In batches, fry the bacon in a large skillet over moderate heat till half-cooked and transfer to a plate. Retain the fat in the skillet.
- In a shallow bowl, whisk together the eggs, milk, and Tabasco till well blended. Place the flour and bread crumbs on separate plates and dust the smelts in the flour. Dip them into the egg mixture, then roll them in the bread crumbs.
- Alternate 3 smelts and 2 pieces of rolled bacon on each of 4 or 5 metal skewers. Add enough oil to the bacon fat in the skillet to measure about 1½ inches and heat till very hot. Lower the skewers with tongs into the fat and fry till the smelts are browned and the bacon fully cooked, about 2 minutes. Drain briefly on paper towels and serve hot.

MAKES 4 TO 5 SERVINGS

twice-cooked chinese bacon

This specialty of China's Szechuan province was introduced to me many years ago by Craig Claiborne's friend Virginia Lee, at a brunch the two gave at Craig's house in East Hampton, on Long Island. Chinese slab bacon, which is meatier than our own, is available cured or uncured (but not smoked) in many Asian markets and online and is utterly delicious when simmered about an hour, then quickly stir-fried with other spicy ingredients (also available in the same markets). Do note that the rind is left on the bacon for the sake of texture (it's not in the least tough once it's been cooked), and that the bacon can be simmered well in advance of the last-minute stir-fry. I like to think this is one way the Chinese were dealing with bacon more than five thousand years ago, and although I doubt it's a dish you'll make a regular habit of serving at brunch, it is a delectable and unusual introduction to authentic Chinese regional cooking—and it's fun to make once in a while. Serve the bacon with fresh fruit and either hot sesame rolls or thick, deep-fried won ton skins (available packaged in many supermarkets).

2 pounds fresh, lean Chinese slab bacon, including the rind
4 medium red bell peppers, seeded and cut into thin strips
4 garlic cloves, crushed
3 tablespoons chile paste (Szechuan paste)
1½ tablespoons bean sauce
2 teaspoons sugar
1 tablespoon dry sherry
½ cup peanut oil
3 scallions (green leaves included), cut into 1-inch lengths

• Place the bacon in a pot with enough water to cover by 1 inch. Bring to a boil, reduce the heat to low, cover, and simmer till the bacon can be pierced with a fork, about 1 hour. Drain, let cool, and slice the meat down through the rind ⅛ inch thick.

• In a large bowl, combine the peppers and garlic, toss, and set aside. In another bowl, combine the chile paste, bean sauce, sugar, and sherry, stir well, and set aside.

• In a wok or large, heavy skillet, heat the oil till hot, add the bacon slices, stir-fry till lightly browned, 7 to 8 minutes, and transfer to a plate. Add the peppers and garlic to the pan, stir-fry 1 minute, and add to the bacon. Add the chile paste mixture to the pan and stir about 1 minute. Return the bacon and peppers and garlic to the pan and stir just till heated through. Add the scallions and stir no more than a few seconds. Serve hot.

MAKES 6 SERVINGS

soups and chowders

chilled edamame and bacon soup

This unusual soup is one of the best ways I know to use the young, green, sweet soybeans called edamame. Steamed or fried, salted, and often eaten as a snack food in Asia, edamame are now not only sold frozen (shelled and unshelled) in most markets but increasingly available fresh in farmers markets during the summer months. The affinity between lima beans (as well as split peas and black-eyed peas) and bacon was established ages ago, and while limas can certainly be substituted for the edamame in this recipe, the more exotic bean does provide a new taste experience that I find very exciting—especially when the soup is chilled and served with either ham biscuits or small finger sandwiches.

6 slices lean streaky bacon
1 medium onion, chopped
2 cups chicken broth
2 cups water
Two 10-ounce packages frozen shelled edamame
Salt and freshly ground black pepper to taste
2 scallions (part of green leaves included), chopped

• In a large skillet, fry the bacon over moderate heat till crisp, drain on paper towels, and crumble. Reserve the bacon fat.

• Heat about 2 tablespoons of the bacon fat in a large, heavy saucepan over moderate heat, add the onion, and stir till softened, about 3 minutes. Add the broth, water, edamame, and salt and pepper, reduce the heat to low, cover, and simmer till the beans are tender, about 10 minutes.

• Transfer the mixture to a food processor, purée, and return it to the pan. Add the bacon, stir well, and heat over moderate heat 5 minutes. Remove the pan from the heat and let the soup cool. Transfer to a bowl, cover with plastic wrap, and chill at least 2 hours. Serve in soup plates and sprinkle chopped scallions over the top of each portion.

MAKES 4 SERVINGS

chicken, corn, and bacon chowder

This smoky chowder is one of the best (and easiest) ways I know to use leftover chicken or turkey. Corncob-smoked bacon, which seems to be primarily a specialty of artisanal producers in Vermont and New Hampshire, has a distinctive robust flavor all its own, and only a couple of slices are needed to transform an otherwise bland soup or chowder into a truly memorable dish. Don't forget: this is a white chowder, meaning the vegetables and flour must be stirred to prevent any browning. If the chowder appears too thick for your taste, simply thin it with a little more milk.

2 thick slices corncob-smoked bacon (or wood-smoked bacon), cut into small pieces
1 small onion, chopped
2 celery ribs, chopped
2 tablespoons all-purpose flour
4 to 5 cups whole milk
2 cups shredded leftover cooked chicken
1 cup peeled and cubed potatoes
One 10-ounce package frozen corn kernels, thawed
Salt and freshly ground black pepper to taste
Cayenne pepper to taste

• In a large, heavy saucepan, fry the bacon over moderate heat till crisp and drain on paper towels. Add the onion and celery to the fat in the pan and stir till the vegetables are softened, about 5 minutes. Add the flour and stir steadily 1 minute longer. Add the milk and bring almost to a boil, stirring. Add the chicken, potatoes, corn, bacon, salt and pepper, and cayenne, reduce the heat to moderate, and simmer till the potatoes are tender, about 10 minutes.

• Serve the chowder hot in soup plates.

MAKES 4 SERVINGS

BACON BUZZ
Bacon consumption in the United States has increased about 40 percent during the past five years. Burger King alone now uses more than five million pounds of bacon per year.

maryland crab, shrimp, and bacon chowder

Virtually any seafood house or restaurant around Chesapeake Bay that serves a crab and/or shrimp chowder is almost sure to flavor it with small pieces of lean bacon (and today, the more serious chefs in the area are likely to use various styles of artisanal bacon). More often than not for chowder, fresh claw crabmeat is preferred to lump backfin, not so much because it's considerably cheaper but because it's much sweeter—even if it's a pain to pick over for shell and cartilage. As for trying to substitute canned or frozen crabmeat (which is stringy and dried out), all I can say is you're courting disaster. Likewise, if you can't find fresh shrimp in the shells (even though it's most likely been previously flash-frozen), forget about making this chowder.

4 slices lean streaky bacon, cut into small pieces
2 medium onions, diced
4 medium potatoes, peeled and diced
1 cup water
7 cups milk
Salt and freshly ground black pepper to taste
¾ pound fresh claw crabmeat, carefully picked over for shells and cartilage
¾ pound small fresh shrimp, peeled and deveined
Sweet paprika, for sprinkling

• In a large, heavy saucepan, fry the bacon over moderate heat and drain on paper towels. Add the onions, potatoes, and water to the fat in the pan, bring to a simmer, cover, and cook till the water has evaporated and the potatoes are tender, 15 to 20 minutes. Add the milk and salt and pepper and return the mixture to the simmer. Add the crabmeat, shrimp, and bacon, return to a simmer, and cook 5 minutes, stirring.
• Serve the chowder in soup plates sprinkled with paprika.

MAKES 6 TO 8 SERVINGS

chicken, ham hock, and bacon chowder

This hearty chowder is not only almost a meal in itself with a tart green salad and good bread but also a perfect way to deal with a flavorful hock sawed off a ham shank and make the most of a whole chicken found on sale. The main secret to its succulence, of course, is the rich, aromatic stock enhanced by bacon, and while no doubt an artisanal one that is dry-cured and carefully smoked is always a tempting option, I've produced delicious chowder using ordinary sugar-cured lean bacon found in all supermarkets. You can use the chicken breast and wings, but the legs and thighs (and odd bits picked from the carcass) have more flavor.

6 slices streaky bacon, cut into 1-inch pieces
One 3½-pound chicken, disjointed
1 small meaty ham hock
1 large onion, studded with 3 cloves
2 celery ribs (leaves included), broken in half
½ teaspoon dried tarragon
½ teaspoon dried thyme
Salt and freshly ground black pepper to taste
3 quarts cold water
2 medium red potatoes
1 medium red bell pepper, seeded and finely diced

• In a large, heavy skillet, fry the bacon over moderate heat till cooked but not crisp and drain on paper towels. Add the chicken pieces to the fat and brown evenly, turning. Meanwhile, in a large, heavy pot, combine the ham hock, onion, celery, tarragon, thyme, salt and pepper, and water and bring to a boil. When the chicken has browned, add it to the pot along with the bacon, return the mixture to a boil, reduce the heat to low, cover, and simmer 1 hour. With a slotted spoon, remove the chicken to a plate and continue simmering the stock for about 45 minutes.

• When cool enough to handle, skin the chicken legs and thighs, remove the meat from the bones, cut into small dice, and reserve the breast and wings for another use. Peel the potatoes and cut into dice. Transfer the ham hock to a cutting board, strain the stock through a fine sieve into another large pot, and discard all the solids. Shred the ham finely and add to the stock. Add the potatoes, bell pepper, and, if the mixture is too thick, more water. Bring to a simmer over moderate heat and cook till the potatoes are just tender, 10 to 15 minutes. Add the chicken, stir well, taste for salt and pepper, and ladle the hot chowder into soup bowls.

MAKES 6 SERVINGS

carolina seafood gumbo

Despite popular perceptions, Louisiana does not have a monopoly on gumbo, this version being just one example of the many gumbos that have been prepared in the coastal Carolina Lowcountry ever since the days of the great rice plantations. What makes this gumbo different from the Creole style is not only the absence of a roux base but the bacon, which is considered absolutely essential to the flavoring. Furthermore, unlike the Louisiana concept, the seafood in this gumbo is purposely overcooked to enrich both the flavor and texture of the dish. Do not use a smoky artisanal bacon, which might overpower the delicate seafood.

4 thick slices slab bacon, rind removed
4 chicken legs or thighs, boned and patted dry with paper towels
2 onions, diced
$\frac{1}{2}$ green bell pepper, seeded and diced
2 garlic cloves, minced
$\frac{1}{4}$ teaspoon dried thyme
Salt and freshly ground black pepper to taste
Tabasco sauce to taste
One 10-ounce package frozen okra, thawed
4 ripe tomatoes, seeded and chopped
2 pounds fresh medium shrimp, shelled and deveined
1 pint fresh shucked oysters, liquor included
1 quart canned clam broth
1 quart water
2 bay leaves
1 lemon, halved and seeded
Buttered boiled rice

• In a large, heavy pot, fry the bacon over moderate heat till crisp, drain on paper towels, and crumble. Add the chicken to the pot, cook on all sides till golden, transfer to a plate, and when cool enough to handle, shred the meat. Add the onion, bell pepper, garlic, thyme, salt and pepper, and Tabasco to the pot, reduce the heat slightly, and cook, stirring, about 3 minutes. Add the okra, stir, and cook another 3 or 4 minutes. Add the bacon, chicken, tomatoes, shrimp, and oysters plus their liquor and stir. Add the broth, water, bay leaves, and lemon halves plus, if necessary, enough additional water to just cover. Simmer, covered, for 2 hours, stirring occasionally.

• Discard the lemon halves and ladle the hot gumbo over rice in deep soup plates or bowls.

MAKES 6 SERVINGS

tomato, basil, and bacon clam chowder

Champions of creamy New England clam chowder who declare pompously that tomatoes have no place in any clam chowder might be more than a little surprised by this amazing version flavored with bacon grease and basil and garnished with crisp, crumbled bacon. While the sturdy chowder does lend itself to experimentation with any number of lightly smoked artisanal bacons, I find that standard streaky bacon that's been carefully sugar-cured is hard to beat. In any case, just be careful not to overcook the clams, which toughens them.

4 thick slices streaky bacon, cut into pieces
1 medium onion, finely chopped
2 celery ribs, finely chopped
3 dozen littleneck clams, shucked and chopped, with liquor reserved
2 cups water
½ cup dry vermouth
1 tablespoon tomato paste
1 medium red potato, peeled and diced
4 medium ripe tomatoes, seeded and chopped
2 tablespoons finely chopped fresh basil leaves
Salt and freshly ground black pepper to taste

• In a 4- to 5-quart pot, fry the bacon over moderate heat till crisp, drain on paper towels, and crumble. Pour all but about 2 tablespoons of fat from the pot, add the onion and celery, and stir till softened, about 5 minutes.

• In a bowl, whisk together 1 cup of the reserved clam liquor, the water, vermouth, and tomato paste and add to the onion mixture. Add the potato, tomatoes, basil, and salt and pepper, stir well, reduce the heat to low, cover, and simmer till the potato is tender, 10 to 15 minutes. Add the clams, stir well, cover, and continue to simmer 2 to 3 minutes. (Do not overcook the clams.)

• To serve, ladle the hot chowder into heavy soup plates or bowls and sprinkle crumbled bacon over the tops.

MAKES 4 SERVINGS

french cabbage, duck gizzard, and bacon soup

One of the most sumptuous and versatile of all French soups, *garbure* is a specialty of both the Béarn region and Gascony and would be inconceivable without the cured, unsmoked bacon known as *ventrèche* (now available from a number of online sources). French cooks might add everything to their soup from roasted red peppers to Swiss chard to grilled chestnuts, but without small white Tarbais beans, some form of preserved duck or goose, and bacon cut from the pork belly or breast, a *garbure* is simply not a *garbure*. Duck gizzard confit is available in jars at speciality food shops and some supermarkets, and our white pea or navy beans (soaked overnight) are best for the velvety texture needed. Slab bacon with equal proportions of fat and lean meat is an acceptable substitute for the *ventrèche*. Although ideally the soup should be prepared 3 or 4 days in advance for the flavors to meld, plan basically on 2 days.

FOR THE BOUILLON
4 chicken legs, disjointed
2 medium onions, cut in half
2 celery ribs, cracked in half
2 turnips, peeled and cut in half
2 carrots, scraped and cut in half
4 peppercorns
Salt to taste
4 quarts water

FOR THE SOUP
1 pound white pea or navy beans, soaked in cold water overnight
1 small green cabbage (blemished leaves discarded), cut into quarters and cored
½ pound *ventrèche* bacon (or slab bacon, rind removed), coarsely chopped
1 garlic clove, smashed
2 pounds (about 4) red potatoes, peeled and quartered
2 pounds duck gizzard confit
Salt and freshly ground black pepper to taste

• To make the bouillon, combine all the ingredients in a large stock pot or Dutch oven, bring to a boil, and skim off the froth. Reduce the heat to low, cover, and simmer for 2 hours. Remove the chicken from the bouillon and reserve for another use. Strain the bouillon into a large bowl, cover, and chill overnight.

• To make the soup the next day, transfer the soaked beans to a large saucepan with enough fresh water to cover, bring to a simmer, cover, and cook 45 minutes. Reserve.

• Plunge the cabbage into a large saucepan of salted boiling water, boil for 10 minutes, and drain. Pour the bouillon into a large pot, add the bacon and garlic, bring to a boil, reduce the heat to low, and simmer 20 minutes. Add the cabbage, potatoes, and carrots, increase the heat slightly, and cook till the vegetables are tender, about 30 minutes. Add the reserved beans, gizzard confit, and salt and pepper and continue to simmer till the beans are meltingly tender, about 45 minutes.

• Serve the soup very hot in heavy, shallow soup bowls.

MAKES 6 TO 8 SERVINGS

BACON BONUS
Since the warmer the room temperature the faster bacon fat can turn rancid, never store a container of fat on the back of the stove; rather, keep it in a cabinet— or, if used infrequently, in the refrigerator.

venetian noodle, white bean, and bacon soup

Pasta con i fagioli e pancetta is a classic noodle, bean, and bacon soup that has been a Venetian specialty for centuries. Since rolls of pancetta are now available in all major markets, it's really a shame not to use it, since it has a distinctive spiciness that's absent in most regular slab bacon. If, however, you're forced to substitute slab bacon, make sure it has enough fat to flavor the soup properly. Since they tend to hold their shape even with lengthy simmering, dried small white pea beans (soaked overnight) are preferable to either navy or Great Northern for this particular soup. (When shopping, notice that some packages of "white beans" contain a mixture of pea beans and navy beans.) This soup is traditionally served warm, not hot.

1½ cups dried white beans, soaked in cold water overnight, drained, and picked over
½ pound pancetta (or slab bacon, rind removed)
1 medium onion, chopped
1 celery rib, chopped
1 medium carrot, scraped and chopped
1 garlic clove, minced
3 parsley sprigs, leaves chopped
1 fresh sage sprig, leaves stripped and chopped (or ¼ teaspoon dried sage)
1 bay leaf
Salt and freshly ground black pepper to taste
6 ounces dried ribbon noodles
2 tablespoons olive oil

• In a heavy 5- to 6-quart pot, combine the beans, pancetta, onion, celery, carrot, garlic, parsley, sage, and bay leaf and add enough water to cover. Bring to a boil, reduce the heat to low, cover, and simmer till the beans are soft, about 2 hours.

• Ladle about 1 cup of the mixture into a blender or food processor and reduce to a purée. Scrape the purée back into the soup, season with salt and pepper, and return to a boil. Add the noodles and boil till they are cooked through but still al dente, about 12 minutes.

• With a slotted spoon, remove the pancetta and cut it into thin strips.

• Before serving, add the olive oil, season with more pepper, and stir well. Serve the soup warm in soup bowls with strips of pancetta scattered over the top.

MAKES 6 SERVINGS

german fennel and bacon soup

Unlike some others, I have an absolute passion for the flavor of licorice, so when my friend and colleague Jean Anderson told me about this creamy, delicate fennel and bacon soup, which, for some reason, I'd never encountered on my travels in Germany, I couldn't get the recipe fast enough. Fennel itself (or, more precisely, the Florence fennel found in most markets) becomes just sweeter and more subtle when cooked, reason enough for German chefs to add both dried fennel seeds and aniseed to the soup to restore the distinctive licorice flavor. (If you don't share this passion, simply ignore the aniseed in the recipe.) For me, the real revelation was the subtle affinity between the fennel and bacon, and while German *Speck* does seem to have a mysteriously wonderful flavor all its own, I've learned that any fine double-smoked bacon produces equally good results in this soup. If you want a more dramatic presentation, use the chopped feathery fennel tops as a garnish instead of stirring them into the soup with the bacon.

1 large fennel bulb (about 1½ pounds)
2 ounces *Speck* (or double-smoked slab bacon), cut into ¼-inch cubes
1 tablespoon butter
2 large onions, coarsely chopped
1 large potato, peeled and coarsely chopped
1 teaspoon fennel seeds
¼ teaspoon aniseed
1 bay leaf
¼ teaspoon ground nutmeg
4 cups chicken broth
1 teaspoon salt
¼ teaspoon freshly ground black pepper
½ cup heavy cream

• Remove, rinse, and dry the feathery fennel tops, chop them moderately fine, and reserve ½ cup of them. Discard any discolored fennel stalks, coarsely chop the remaining stalks, and set aside.

• In a large pot, fry the bacon over moderate heat till crisp and drain on paper towels. Melt the butter in the bacon fat, add the onion, chopped fennel stalks, potato, fennel seeds, aniseed, bay leaf, and nutmeg and stir about 2 minutes. Reduce the heat to low, cover, and steam about 15 minutes. Add the broth, bring to a low simmer, cover, and cook till the vegetables are very soft, about 1½ hours. Remove and discard the bay leaf. Cool the mixture, then, in batches, purée it in a food processor.

• Return the mixture to the pot, add the salt, pepper, and cream, and bring to a low simmer. Stir in the fennel tops and bacon, then ladle the hot soup into soup plates or bowls.

MAKES 6 SERVINGS

austrian lentil and bacon soup

Only Hungarian cooks use more bacon in their hearty soups than Germans and Austrians do, and perhaps the most beloved Austrian classic is this thick lentil one bursting with smoky *Speck* and flavorful frankfurters, like one I had not long ago in Dürnstein while cruising the Danube. In Austrian country restaurants and *Stuben,* I've listened more than once to heated debate over whether genuine *Linsensuppe* should contain a little vinegar to counter the other rich ingredients. I think about two tablespoons helps to create just the right balance, but you may want to add a bit more during the final simmer. Serve this soup during the winter with a big bowl of red cabbage coleslaw, a loaf of dark pumpernickel bread, and, of course, steins of frothy lager.

½ **pound smoked slab bacon (preferably *Speck*), rind removed**
2 **quarts water**
2 **cups dried quick-cooking lentils, rinsed**
1 **medium leek (part of light green leaves included), finely chopped**
1 **celery rib, finely chopped**
1 **large carrot, scraped and finely chopped**
2 **medium onions, finely chopped**
2 **tablespoons all-purpose flour**
2 **tablespoons cider vinegar**
Salt and freshly ground black pepper to taste
2 **frankfurters, sliced into** ¼**-inch rounds**

• Cut 2 slices from the bacon slab and set the slab aside on a plate. In a large skillet, fry the bacon slices till they render their fat, transfer the slices to a plate, and set the skillet of fat aside.

• In a heavy 4- to 5-quart pot or casserole, bring the water to a boil. Add the lentils, the slab and slices of cooked bacon, and the leek, celery, and carrot. Return to a boil, reduce the heat to low, cover, and simmer for 30 minutes.

• Heat the fat in the skillet over moderate heat, add the onion, and stir till softened, about 5 minutes. Sprinkle the flour over the onion, reduce the heat to low, and stir till the flour is golden brown. Ladle about ½ cup of the lentil soup into the skillet and whisk till the mixture is thick and smooth. Add the vinegar and salt and pepper and stir well. Scrape the contents of the skillet into the lentil soup, stir well, cover, and simmer till the lentils are tender, about 30 minutes.

• With a slotted spoon, remove the bacon to a cutting surface, cut into small dice, and return it to the soup with the frankfurter rounds. Simmer about 5 minutes longer and serve the soup hot in heavy soup bowls.

MAKES 6 SERVINGS

hungarian egg noodle, sauerkraut, and gypsy bacon soup

Hungary has a long tradition of homemade noodles, the most popular of which are egg noodles (also called egg barley) that are cut, pinched, rolled, or grated for any number of lusty soups and casseroles. (Dried Hungarian egg noodles are now available in the pasta section of most markets.) Genuine Hungarian gypsy bacon, spiced, cured with pig's blood, and smoked to a reddish color, can sometimes be found in Hungarian or German meat markets or online, but if it's difficult to locate, substitute a good paprika bacon, available in many markets or from various online sources. (Ironically, when a slab of bacon cooked over an open fire in Hungary is overcooked and charred, it is often referred to disparagingly as "gypsy bacon.") When preparing this soup, test the bacon after the hour of simmering: if it's not fully tender, simmer the soup up to 30 minutes longer.

½ pound sliced Hungarian gypsy or paprika bacon, cut into pieces
1 cup dried Hungarian egg noodles
1 medium onion, chopped
1 small green bell pepper, seeded and chopped
1 garlic clove, chopped
1½ tablespoons all-purpose flour
1½ tablespoons sweet Hungarian paprika
4 cups beef broth
1 pound packaged sauerkraut, rinsed, drained, and finely chopped
½ teaspoon dried marjoram
Salt and freshly ground black pepper to taste
4 cups water

• In a heavy 6-quart pot, fry the bacon over moderate heat till almost crisp and drain on paper towels. Pour off all but about 2 tablespoons of fat from the pot, add the noodles, and stir till they begin to color, about 2 minutes. Add the onion, bell pepper, and garlic and stir till the vegetables soften and the noodles are golden, about 3 minutes. Sprinkle the flour and paprika over the top, stir, add 1 cup of the broth, and stir about 1 minute longer. Add the sauerkraut, bacon, marjoram, salt and pepper, the remaining broth, and the water, stir, and bring to a boil. Reduce the heat to low, cover, and simmer for 1 hour.

• To serve, ladle the hot soup into heavy soup bowls.

MAKES 6 SERVINGS

russian borscht

Virtually the national dish of the Ukraine, borscht is traditionally made with a flavorful secondary cut of beef and either pork shoulder or a meaty smoked bacon—or both. Some Russian cooks add a teaspoon or so of sugar to counteract the acidity of the beets and tomatoes, but personally I like the tartness. If you prefer to serve the soup chilled instead of hot, be sure to skim off any fat that forms on the surface. Although it is customary to garnish a bowl of borscht with a dollop of sour cream, I like mine plain. What is obligatory with the soup are thin slices of dark pumpernickel bread—buttered.

2 pounds boned beef chuck, trimmed of excess fat and cut into 1-inch cubes
¼ pound double-smoked lean slab bacon, rind removed, cut into 1-inch cubes
2 quarts water
1 garlic clove, minced
1 teaspoon salt
Freshly ground black pepper to taste
1 bay leaf, crumbled
1 medium onion, coarsely chopped
1 celery rib, coarsely chopped
1 carrot, scraped and coarsely chopped
4 medium canned beets, diced
One 14½-ounce can diced tomatoes, juice included
2 cups finely shredded green cabbage
1 medium potato, peeled and diced
2 tablespoons red wine vinegar
1 tablespoon snipped fresh dill
Sour cream, for garnish (optional)

• In a large pot, combine the beef, bacon, water, garlic, salt, pepper, bay leaf, and onion, bring to a boil, and skim froth from the top. Reduce the heat to low, cover, and simmer till the beef is tender, about 2 hours. Add the celery and carrot and simmer about 20 minutes longer. Add the beets, tomatoes, and cabbage and simmer 20 minutes longer. Add the potato, vinegar, and dill and simmer about 15 minutes longer.

• Serve the soup hot or chilled in deep soup bowls, with or without a dollop of sour cream on top.

MAKES 6 SERVINGS

serbian bacon, bean, and cabbage soup

If anyone loves and uses more bacon in soups than the Germans and Hungarians, it's the Serbians. (I have a close Serbian friend who relishes nothing more than eating raw bacon!) Simple and very easy to prepare, this classic soup derives much of its succulence from the way the bacon virtually melts while simmering with the other ingredients, so be sure to fry it initially only till it renders enough fat in which to cook the onions and garlic. While any double-smoked bacon is appropriate for this soup, the ideal would be an amazingly mellow, beechwood-smoked German *Speck* often found in upscale meat markets and delis or ordered online.

½ pound thick-sliced, double-smoked bacon, cut into pieces
2 medium onions, chopped
2 garlic cloves, minced
1 medium head green cabbage (discolored outer leaves removed), cored and chopped
One 19-ounce can Great Northern beans, drained
1 large bunch parsley leaves, chopped
6 cups chicken broth
Salt and freshly ground black pepper to taste

• In a heavy 6-quart pot, fry the bacon over moderate heat just till it renders about half of its fat and transfer to a plate. Add the onion and garlic to the fat and stir till softened, about 5 minutes. Add the cabbage, beans, parsley, bacon, broth, and salt and pepper, stir well, reduce the heat to low, cover, and simmer till the cabbage is very tender, about 45 minutes.

• To serve, ladle the hot soup into heavy soup bowls.

MAKES 6 SERVINGS

BACON BUZZ
German curing and smoking techniques were introduced to America by Pennsylvania Dutch settlers in the 1830s.

mexican squash, yam, and bacon soup

Mexican cooks use bacon not only to flavor but to garnish numerous robust soups like this squash and yam one from the Oaxaca region. If you can find genuine round, pale green *criollo* squash in a Hispanic market, by all means use it in place of the butternut or acorn variety, along with its tasty shoots and tendrils. (In Mexico, even the squash seeds would be dried or toasted and added to the soup.) Likewise, look for brown- or purple-skin *camotes,* which are true yams indigenous to Latin and South America that are all too often confused with our sweet potatoes. Since most squash is pretty bland, it's easy to understand why this soup calls for an intense, smoky bacon to give it real character. You might, in fact, even add a couple more slices—as I tend to do.

One 2- to 3-pound butternut or acorn squash
2 sweet potatoes
3 thick slices double-smoked bacon, cut into small pieces
1 medium onion, chopped
2 garlic cloves, chopped
6 cups chicken broth
Salt and freshly ground black pepper to taste
Chopped fresh chives, for garnish

• Preheat the oven to 425°F.
• With a large, heavy knife, cut the squash in half lengthwise and place cut sides up in a baking pan with the sweet potatoes. Roast till the squash and sweet potatoes are fork tender, about 1 hour, then scoop out the flesh from both and reserve in a bowl.
• In a skillet, fry the bacon till crisp and drain on paper towels. Transfer about 2 tablespoons of the bacon fat to a large pot over moderate heat, add the onion and garlic, and stir till softened, about 5 minutes. Add the reserved squash and sweet potatoes, broth, and salt and pepper, stir, and cook about 30 minutes.
• Transfer the mixture to a blender or food processor, purée, and return soup to the pot. Add half the bacon, stir over moderate heat about 2 minutes, and adjust the seasoning. Ladle the hot soup into soup bowls and garnish the tops with the remaining bacon pieces and a sprinkling of chives.

MAKES 6 SERVINGS

ecuadorian smoky pumpkin soup

Throughout Ecuador (and much of Latin America), wholesome soups are at the heart of almost every meal, and none is more beloved than those made with the large, oval, indigenous "green pumpkin" known as *calabaza* (or *zapallo*) and flavored with a smoky bacon. These flavorful winter squash with bright orange flesh are often available in Latin American or Caribbean markets, but if you can't find them, I've learned that either ordinary pumpkins that are not too ripe or Hubbard squash are perfectly acceptable for this luscious soup spiked with a superior dark rum like Myers's. Some might think the soup needs the added intensity of double-smoked bacon, but personally I'm quite satisfied with regular hickory- or applewood-smoked. And if you want a dramatic presentation, scoop out all the remaining flesh of the pumpkin for another use and serve the piping hot soup in the pumpkin shell.

One 6- to 7-pound pumpkin
6 slices streaky smoked bacon
2 medium onions, chopped
2 garlic cloves, minced
1 teaspoon dried ground sage
Tabasco sauce to taste
Salt and freshly ground black pepper to taste
4 cups chicken broth
3 cups half-and-half
2 to 3 tablespoons dark rum

• Cut a wide, deep circle around the stem of the pumpkin and remove the lid. Scrape the seeds and stringy membranes from the pumpkin with a large, heavy spoon and discard, then scrape out most of the flesh remaining in the pumpkin and place on a work surface. Coarsely chop enough of the flesh to measure 4 cups and reserve the remaining flesh for another use.

• In a large saucepan or pot, fry the bacon till crisp, drain on paper towels, and crumble. Add the onions and garlic to the pan and cook over moderate heat for 3 minutes, stirring. Add the chopped pumpkin and sage, season with Tabasco and salt and pepper, and stir. Add the broth, stir, cover, and simmer over moderately low heat till the pumpkin is tender, about 30 minutes. Remove from the heat and let cool.

• Transfer the contents of the pan to a blender or food processor (in batches), reduce to a purée, and transfer back to the pan. Add the half-and-half, crumbled bacon, and rum, stir well, and heat till very hot but not boiling.

• Serve the hot soup in wide soup plates.

MAKES 6 TO 8 SERVINGS

pot sticker, shiitake mushroom, and chinese bacon soup

Given the fact that the Chinese were most likely the first to dry-cure bacon, I like to think that this extraordinary soup has been around at least a few thousand years. Pot stickers (or Chinese dumplings) are simply wonton skins filled with ground meat or seafood and seasonings, and they can be found frozen in packages at most markets. If you can find dried, dark wood-ear mushrooms in an Asian market, they have considerably more flavor than the shiitakes, but be warned that they swell about five times in size when soaked in water. Look also for genuine Chinese cabbage (*petsai*), which is sweeter and more delicate than ordinary green cabbage; otherwise, use Savoy cabbage. You may be lucky to find a long piece of Chinese bacon that has been hydrated and sliced, but since most are hard from having been air-dried, you'll have to soak it in water at least 6 or 7 hours before slicing. Also, be sure to remove any rind from the bacon.

3 thick slices Chinese bacon (or double-smoked bacon), cut into small pieces
One 1-pound package frozen pot stickers stuffed with ground meat or seafood, thawed
6 cups chicken broth
1 small head Chinese cabbage (or Savoy cabbage), shredded
2 cups sliced fresh shiitake mushroom caps
1 cup scraped, thickly shredded carrots
⅔ cup chopped scallions (part of green leaves included)
1 teaspoon sesame oil
Salt and freshly ground black pepper to taste

• In a skillet, fry the bacon over moderate heat till just softened and set aside.

• Bring an 8-quart pot of water to a boil, add the pot stickers, and boil, uncovered, till cooked through, 6 to 8 minutes, stirring gently from time to time. Remove from the heat and keep the dumplings warm in the water.

• Meanwhile, in another large, heavy pot, bring the broth to a boil, add the cabbage, mushrooms, carrots, and reserved bacon, reduce the heat to moderate, and cook 8 to 10 minutes. Add the scallions, sesame oil, and salt and pepper, and continue cooking till the vegetables are just tender, 3 to 5 minutes.

• To serve, lift the pot stickers from the water with a slotted spoon, divide them among 4 soup bowls, and ladle equal amounts of the soup over the tops. Serve hot.

MAKES 4 SERVINGS

salads and sandwiches

wilted spinach and avocado salad with warm bacon dressing

This classic American salad would be almost inconceivable without both bacon and the sour-sweet hot bacon grease dressing needed to wilt the spinach. You are certainly free to experiment with a special artisanal bacon for the salad, but personally I'm quite satisfied with any of the top-quality, lightly smoked streaky bacon with equal proportions of fat and lean meat widely available in supermarkets. I do suggest you try to find young, crisp, "baby" spinach, avoiding any that is limp or has tough leaves or yellow spots.

¼ cup cider vinegar
1 teaspoon Dijon mustard
1 teaspoon sugar
1 garlic clove, minced
Salt and freshly ground black pepper to taste
½ pound fresh spinach, stemmed, rinsed, and patted dry
1 ripe avocado, peeled, seeded, and diced
½ red onion, thinly sliced
8 thick slices lean streaky bacon
½ cup extra-virgin olive oil
2 hard-boiled eggs, coarsely chopped

• In a small bowl, combine the vinegar and mustard and whisk till well blended. Add the sugar, garlic, and salt and pepper, stir well, and set aside.

• In a large salad bowl, combine the spinach, avocado, and onion and set aside.

• In a large skillet, fry the bacon over moderate heat till crisp, drain on paper towels, and crumble coarsely. Pour off all but about 2 tablespoons of grease from the skillet, add the oil plus the vinegar-mustard mixture, and stir till the dressing is hot. Pour the dressing over the spinach mixture and toss well. Add the bacon and eggs, toss well again, and taste for seasoning. Serve the salad immediately on wide salad plates.

MAKES 4 SERVINGS

iceberg wedges with bacon, blue cheese, and buttermilk dressing

Just in the past couple of years, this classic combo, long disparaged by fatuous food snobs, has made a big comeback even in fancy restaurants. And why not? Thomas Jefferson relished nothing more than a well-dressed wedge of "tennis ball lettuce," ancestor of our iceberg. And when today's crisp, tender lettuce is cloaked in a silky buttermilk dressing redolent of peppery bacon and zesty blue cheese, the salad has true pedigree. Since the bacon, blue cheese, and mayo are all salty, absolutely no seasoning is necessary. I like to serve these wedges with ham biscuits or sesame sticks.

½ pound thick peppered bacon slices, cut into 1-inch pieces
1¼ cups mayonnaise
¼ cup buttermilk
1 tablespoon red wine vinegar
Tabasco sauce to taste
1 cup crumbled blue cheese
1 large, firm head iceberg lettuce, wilted leaves discarded, partly cored, and cut into 4 wedges
1 small red onion, thinly sliced

- In a large skillet, fry the bacon over moderate heat till almost crisp and drain on paper towels.
- In a bowl, combine the mayonnaise, buttermilk, vinegar, and Tabasco and stir till well blended. Add the bacon and blue cheese and gently stir till well blended. Chill the dressing about 30 minutes.
- Arrange the lettuce wedges on salad plates, spoon equal amounts of dressing over the tops, and garnish with the onion slices.

MAKES 4 SERVINGS

BACON BUZZ
The finest American bacon is produced from hogs raised to specification in Iowa, North Carolina, and North and South Dakota, fed on barley and corn, and slaughtered at certain weights.

cobb salad

Created in 1936 by Robert Cobb at The Brown Derby restaurant in Hollywood (supposedly from leftovers in the kitchen), the Cobb salad is not only one of America's great contributions to world gastronomy but also a dish that would be virtually pointless without bacon. Of course, over the decades, the salad has been subjected to every abuse imaginable, but even when I've been exposed to "innovative" versions that make me cringe, I've yet to encounter a Cobb that didn't contain at least a few strips of crumbled bacon. No doubt the original boasted little more than ordinary streaky bacon. This is just fine, but it's also true that no salad lends itself more to experimentation with all the new styles of imported and artisanal bacon that have come on the market in recent years.

6 slices thick hickory-smoked bacon
2 whole chicken breasts, split
2 scallions (part of green leaves included), cut into pieces
1 celery rib, cut in half
1 bay leaf
6 peppercorns
4 cups chicken broth
Salt and freshly ground black pepper to taste
1 bunch watercress (tough stems removed), rinsed, dried, and chilled
½ head romaine lettuce, rinsed, dried, and chilled
½ head iceberg lettuce, chilled
4 large hard-boiled eggs, coarsely chopped
2 ripe avocados, peeled, seeded, diced, and sprinkled with lemon juice
2 ripe medium tomatoes, peeled, seeded, and coarsely chopped
2 ounces Roquefort or blue cheese, crumbled
3 tablespoons chopped fresh chives
½ cup red wine vinegar
1 teaspoon dry mustard
1 teaspoon Worcestershire sauce
1 cup olive oil

- In a large skillet, fry the bacon over moderate heat till crisp, drain on paper towels, and crumble.
- Arrange the chicken breasts in a large, deep skillet or medium baking pan and add the scallions, celery, bay leaf, peppercorns, broth, salt and pepper, and just enough water to cover, if necessary. Bring to a boil, reduce the heat to low, and poach the chicken at the barest simmer for 15 minutes. Remove from the heat and let cool in the broth.

• With a slotted spoon, transfer the chicken to a work surface. Discard the skin and bones, cut the meat into ½-inch cubes, and place in a large mixing bowl. Pull or shred the greens into bite-size pieces and add to the chicken. Add the eggs, avocado, tomatoes, bacon, cheese, and chives and toss till well blended.

• In a small bowl, whisk together the vinegar, mustard, Worcestershire, and salt and pepper to taste. Whisk in the oil till thoroughly incorporated, pour the dressing over the salad, and toss till the ingredients are well coated. To serve, mound the salad across a serving platter or divide equally among individual salad plates.

MAKES 6 SERVINGS

BACON BUZZ
During westward expansion in the United States in the nineteenth century, settlers making the four-month trek from Missouri to California normally included in their provisions about twenty-five pounds of bacon per person.

southern shrimp and pea salad with cracklings

I created this summer salad years ago at a beach in South Carolina, and if I say so myself, it is truly sumptuous. At the time, I used ordinary slab bacon to make the cracklings, but today I might well substitute an artisanal one that is wood-smoked or peppered, or even an elegant honey-cured bacon. Whichever you choose, just remember that the bacon should be fatty enough to produce crisp cracklings. Freshly boiled shrimp are obligatory for this salad, and while you can use frozen peas, fresh ones (boiled till just barely tender) make all the difference. With the salad, you need serve only cornbread, hot biscuits, or crisp bread sticks.

½ pound fatty peppered bacon (or fatty, lightly smoked slab bacon), diced
2 pounds fresh medium shrimp
½ lemon
2½ cups cooked peas
2 small dill pickles, diced
1 cup mayonnaise
3 tablespoons fresh lemon juice
2 tablespoons heavy cream
1 teaspoon prepared horseradish
Salt and freshly ground black pepper to taste
Leaves of chicory (curly endive), rinsed and dried
2 ripe medium tomatoes, quartered
3 large hard-boiled eggs, shelled and quartered

• In a large, heavy skillet, render the diced bacon over low heat for 20 to 30 minutes or till crisp and golden brown, watching carefully to prevent burning. Drain the cracklings on paper towels and set aside.

• Place the shrimp in a large saucepan. Squeeze the lemon half over the shrimp and drop it in the pot. Add enough water to cover, bring to a boil, remove from the heat, let stand for 1 minute, and drain. When cool enough to handle, shell, devein, and place the shrimp in a large mixing bowl. Add the peas and diced pickles, toss well, cover with plastic wrap, and chill for 1 hour.

• In a small bowl, whisk together the mayonnaise, lemon juice, heavy cream, horseradish, and salt and pepper, add the dressing to the shrimp and pea mixture, and toss well. Line a large salad bowl with chicory leaves, mound the salad in the middle, sprinkle the cracklings over the top, and garnish the sides with the tomatoes and eggs. Serve the salad on wide salad plates.

MAKES 4 TO 6 SERVINGS

chicken, avocado, and orange salad with bacon dressing

This is one of the most beguiling summer salads I know, all thanks to the way bacon and bacon grease do wonders to enhance the flavor of the main ingredients. If you like, the orange sections can be halved and tossed with the other ingredients instead of being used as a garnish, and for a more exotic salad, you might use tangy-sweet, red-fleshed, seedless clementines, if they're available. This bacon dressing contains no oil, so if you insist on a dressing with more body, whisk in a little extra-virgin olive oil or sunflower oil to taste.

6 slices streaky bacon
3 scallions (part of green tops included), minced
½ cup balsamic vinegar
½ cup water
2 teaspoons Dijon mustard
1½ cups shredded escarole
1½ cups shredded Boston lettuce
1 cup shredded arugula
4 cups cubed cooked chicken breasts
2 small ripe avocados, peeled, seeded, and cubed
2 large hard-boiled eggs, shelled and cut into large dice
1 teaspoon fresh lemon juice
Salt and freshly ground black pepper to taste
2 oranges

• In a large skillet, fry the bacon over moderate heat till crisp, drain on paper towels, and crumble. Pour 2 to 3 tablespoons of the bacon grease into a saucepan, add the scallions, and stir over moderate heat 1 minute. Add the vinegar, water, and mustard, whisk till the mustard is well incorporated, continue stirring about 3 minutes, and set the dressing aside.

• In a large mixing bowl, combine the greens, chicken, avocados, eggs, lemon juice, and salt and pepper and toss well. Cut the oranges in half and remove the sections with a citrus knife, avoiding as much membrane as possible. Add the sections to the salad and toss again. Chill the salad for about 30 minutes.

• When ready to serve, pour the dressing over the salad, sprinkle the crumbled bacon over the top, toss to blend thoroughly, and serve on wide salad plates.

MAKES 6 SERVINGS

french chicory, beet, and bacon salad

Every chef in Lyon, France, has his or her version of *frisée* salad (some including diced new potatoes, soft-boiled eggs, and various other meats), but leave it to the great Paul Bocuse to come up with this unusual one featuring a julienne of boiled beets and *lardons* of smoky slab bacon, which he and I shared one day at a late lunch in his restaurant. In Lyon, I've had *frisée* salads made with smoked and unsmoked pork belly (*lard fumé* and *ventrèche*), fried salt pork (*lard salé*), and even toothy cured bacon rind (*couenne*), so feel free to experiment with all types of bacon. Traditionally, a *frisée* is eaten with crusty bread, crisp thin french fries, and chilled Beaujolais.

1 pound beets
1 head chicory (curly endive), rinsed, dried, and torn into pieces
½ pound lean slab bacon (rind removed), diced
½ cup walnut oil
2 garlic cloves, finely chopped
¼ cup red wine vinegar
2 tablespoons mixed chopped fresh herbs (or 2 teaspoons dried)
Salt and freshly ground black pepper to taste

• Trim off all but 2 inches of the beet tops and leave on the root ends. Scrub the beets gently, taking care not to break the skins, and place in a large saucepan with enough water to cover. Bring to a boil, reduce the heat slightly, and boil for 20 minutes. Drain the beets, plunge them into a pot of cold water for 2 minutes, remove the skins and root ends, and cut into julienne.

• In a large salad bowl, combine the beets and chicory and toss.

• In a skillet, fry the bacon over moderate heat till half-cooked and drain off the grease. Add the oil and garlic to the skillet, continue frying the bacon till almost crisp, and add the contents of the skillet to the beets and chicory. Add the vinegar to the skillet, swirl it around till well heated, and pour it over the salad. Add the herbs and salt and pepper, toss well, and serve immediately.

MAKES 6 SERVINGS

italian tuna, white bean, and bacon salad

This luscious salad is found in trattorias all over Italy, and one reason it's so memorable is because most chefs use the superior tuna belly packed in olive oil called *ventresca*. It is possible to find genuine (and expensive) *ventresca* tuna in our finer markets, but if it's not available, there's nothing wrong with a reliable domestic brand of solid white albacore packed in oil. (Don't even think of using insipid tuna packed in water for this salad.) Ditto domestic pancetta, which is now often just as good as the imported bacon. While cannellini, which are white Italian kidney beans, are available both dried and canned, I find the latter too soft for this salad and substitute white pea beans when I can't find the dried Italian.

½ pound dried cannellini beans (or dried white pea beans)
2 garlic cloves, peeled and crushed
2 fresh sage leaves
6 ounces pancetta, diced
Two 6-ounce cans solid white albacore tuna packed in oil, drained
1 small red onion, thinly sliced
2 tablespoon minced fresh chives
Extra-virgin olive oil to taste
1 tablespoon red wine vinegar
Salt and freshly ground black pepper to taste

• Place the beans in a large bowl, add enough cold water to cover, and let soak at least 6 hours or overnight.

• Drain the beans, transfer to a large pot, add enough fresh water to cover, and add the garlic and sage. Bring to a low boil, reduce the heat to low, cover, and simmer till the beans are tender, about 1 hour. Drain and let cool.

• In a medium skillet, lightly brown the pancetta over moderate heat and drain on paper towels.

• Transfer the beans to a large serving bowl and add the pancetta, tuna, onion, and chives. Drizzle olive oil and vinegar over the top, season with salt and pepper, and toss gently with a wooden spoon and fork till well blended, carefully breaking up any large chunks of tuna. Cover with plastic wrap and chill the salad about 1 hour before serving.

MAKES 4 SERVINGS

french green lentil and bacon salad

Green lentils are lighter, less starchy, and more flavorful than the more ordinary brown ones, and for centuries, the finest and most sought-after green variety (*lentilles du Puy*) has flourished in the volcanic soil of France's Auvergne region. Once was the time when only dried, expensive French green lentils were available in the United States, but now that they're grown here and cost a lot less, it's a cinch to replicate this delectable salad found all over the central provinces of France. The bacon most French chefs would use is unsmoked *ventrèche,* but when that's not easy to come by, I don't hesitate a second to use the more readily available pancetta or even meaty salt pork ("streak-o'-lean" in the South). Although green lentils do hold their shape much better than other varieties, be careful to cook them just till they're tender.

2 cups French green lentils, rinsed and picked over
6 cups water
1 bay leaf
Salt to taste
½ pound French *ventrèche* bacon (or slab bacon, rind removed), cut into ½-inch pieces
1 medium onion, chopped
2 celery ribs, diced
2 garlic cloves, minced
½ teaspoon dried thyme
¼ cup red wine vinegar
2 tablespoons Dijon mustard
Freshly ground black pepper to taste
½ cup French olive oil
3 tablespoons finely chopped fresh parsley leaves

• In a large saucepan, combine the lentils, water, bay leaf, and salt. Bring to a boil, reduce the heat to low, cover, and simmer till the lentils are tender but not falling apart, 15 to 20 minutes. Remove from the heat.

• In a large skillet, fry the bacon over moderate heat till almost crisp and drain on paper towels. Pour off all but about 2 tablespoons of fat from the skillet, add the onion, celery, garlic, thyme, and salt to taste, and stir till the vegetables are softened, about 5 minutes. Remove pan from the heat.

• In a bowl, combine the vinegar, mustard, and pepper and whisk till well blended. Gradually add the oil, whisking till the vinaigrette is well blended.

• Drain the lentils and discard the bay leaf. Add the bacon, vegetable mixture, and vinaigrette to the pan, bring to a low simmer, and cook just till heated through. Add the parsley, stir well, taste for seasoning, and serve the salad warm on large salad plates or in shallow soup bowls.

MAKES 4 SERVINGS

jamaican smoked fish, cheese, and bacon salad

At the billfish tournament held every fall in Port Antonio on Jamaica's north coast, there's not one restaurant or seafood hut that doesn't offer at least one elaborate salad featuring smoked swordfish, marlin, or other game fish, often teamed with fried, uncured pork belly or a mildly cured bacon produced from the island's large hog population. Some variety of smoked fish is always available in our finer seafood markets, and what I prefer for this salad is smoked haddock. For obvious reasons, use only a sugar-cured, unsmoked streaky bacon, never a highly smoked one.

6 ounces sliced lean sugar-cured streaky bacon
2 pounds smoked fish (cod, haddock, or salmon)
8 cups mixed salad greens torn into bite-size pieces
1 medium red onion, thinly sliced
4 ounces Swiss cheese, cut into julienne
8 ripe cherry tomatoes, cut in half
½ cup mayonnaise
2 tablespoons fresh lemon juice
Freshly ground black pepper to taste

• In a large skillet, fry the bacon over moderate heat till crisp, drain on paper towels, and crumble.

• Remove and discard all skin and bones from the fish, then flake the flesh into a large bowl. Add the greens, onion, cheese, and tomatoes, toss, cover with plastic wrap, and chill about 1 hour.

• In a small bowl, combine the mayonnaise, lemon juice, and pepper and whisk till the dressing is well blended. Add the bacon to the salad, pour the dressing over the top, and toss lightly. Serve on large salad plates.

MAKES 6 SERVINGS

viennese bean, egg, and bacon salad

Canned or dried white, yellow, or purplish beans are commonly combined with bacon throughout Austria, Germany, and Hungary to make numerous soups, stews, and salads like this rather elegant one I encountered at a delightful café in Vienna, while taking a cruise down the Danube to learn more about the cooking in that area of the world. Actually, the smoky bacon seemed to be more like cubes of *lardons* rendered till very crisp, or maybe Hungarian gypsy bacon, so feel free to experiment with various styles. When I asked the waitress about the unusual egg mixture on top of my individual salad, she gave me a strange look and informed me almost indignantly that this is what made the salad a Viennese specialty. If you choose to use dried Great Northern, navy, or pea beans instead of the canned, remember that you must first soak them at least 6 hours in water, then boil them about 1½ hours or till just tender.

One 16-ounce can Great Northern white beans, drained
1 small red onion, chopped
3 tablespoons olive oil
2 tablespoons red wine vinegar
¼ teaspoon salt
Pinch of dried summer savory
Freshly ground black pepper to taste
3 thick lean slices streaky bacon (or slab bacon, rind removed)
2 large hard-boiled eggs, chopped
3 tablespoons mayonnaise
1 teaspoon cider vinegar
1 teaspoon dark grainy mustard
Boston lettuce leaves
Sweet paprika, for sprinkling

• In a bowl, combine the beans and onion. In another small bowl, whisk together the olive oil, red wine vinegar, salt, summer savory, and pepper till well blended, pour over the beans and onions, toss, cover with plastic wrap, and chill 2 hours.

• In a skillet, fry the bacon over moderate heat till crisp, drain on paper towels, and crumble.

• In a small bowl, combine the eggs, mayonnaise, cider vinegar, and mustard and stir till well blended. Drain the bean mixture, add the bacon, and toss. Transfer to a large salad bowl lined with lettuce leaves, spoon the egg mixture over the top, and sprinkle with paprika. Serve the salad chilled or at room temperature.

MAKES 4 APPETIZER SERVINGS OR 2 MAIN-COURSE SERVINGS

german red cabbage and bacon salad

Bacon is a prime ingredient in dozens of German composed salads, and no style is more relished than a mellow *Geräucherterspeck,* with its distinctive smoky beechwood flavor. The closest equivalent in this country is slab bacon double-smoked over applewood chips, available from any number of artisanal producers. Red cabbage, bacon, and caraway seed salad is a German classic found in most country *Stuben,* but chefs might also add a few diced apples, mushrooms, boiled beets, radishes, or grated horseradish. By all means experiment and adjust, but do remember that most German salads have a slightly sweet edge.

4 ounces double-smoked slab bacon (rind removed), cut into ¼-inch cubes
1 medium head red cabbage (about 1½ pounds), cored and shredded
⅓ cup dry red wine
2 tablespoons white vinegar
1 tablespoon sugar
3 tablespoons sunflower oil
2 teaspoons caraway seeds
2 teaspoons salt
Freshly ground black pepper to taste

- In a skillet, fry the bacon over moderate heat till crisp and drain on paper towels.
- Place the cabbage in a large bowl.
- In a small saucepan, combine the wine, vinegar, and sugar, bring to a low boil, and stir till the sugar has dissolved. Pour over the cabbage. Add the oil, caraway seeds, salt, and pepper to the cabbage and toss till well blended. Add the bacon, toss lightly, and serve on wide salad plates.

MAKES 4 TO 6 SERVINGS

BACON BUZZ
During World War II, it was considered patriotic not only to have coffee cans of bacon fat ready for cooking but also to contribute any extra fat to the war effort to help make explosives.

canadian bacon croques-monsieur

A traditional French *croque-monsieur* is made with a rather bland baked ham known as *jambon de Paris,* but when you substitute sliced rounds of fine Canadian bacon, the sandwich takes on a much more distinctive character. Depending on the size of the bacon roll, you may want to use more overlapping slices for each sandwich; just make sure the slices are not too thick. And for extra-rich sandwiches, allow them to soak in the egg wash about 1 minute on each side while the butter is heating in the skillet. A perfect *croque-monsieur* should be just golden brown on the outside, and the sandwich is always eaten with a knife and fork—preferably with a vinegary green salad.

Dijon mustard
8 thin slices pullman-style white bread, or other firm white loaf bread, crusts removed
8 ounces Gruyère cheese, grated
4 slices Canadian bacon
Ground nutmeg to taste
4 tablespoons (½ stick) butter
4 large eggs beaten with 2 tablespoons water in a wide bowl

• Spread mustard evenly over one side of each bread slice and sprinkle half the cheese evenly over 4 of the slices. Place a slice of bacon on the 4 cheese-sprinkled bread slices, sprinkle the remaining cheese evenly over the bacon slices, season each with nutmeg and pepper, and top with the remaining 4 bread slices.

• In a large, heavy skillet or griddle, melt 2 tablespoons of the butter over moderately low heat. Carefully dip both sides of 2 sandwiches into the prepared egg wash, and, using a spatula and fork, place them in the skillet and cook about 4 minutes on each side or till the cheese begins to melt and the outsides are golden brown. Transfer the sandwiches to a hot plate and repeat procedure with the 2 remaining sandwiches.

• Serve the sandwiches hot with knives and forks.

MAKES 4 SERVINGS

the all-american blt sandwich

A favorite at lunch counters, the pride of hotel coffee shops, and a staple in many a school lunch box, the all-American BLT has been around for at least a century and emulated in one form or another all over the globe. Simplicity itself, a great BLT depends only on the finest ingredients: the freshest bread, the best mayo, sun-ripened tomatoes, crisp but tender iceberg lettuce (and only iceberg!), and a truly splendid bacon. Possibly no bacon dish on earth so openly displays the meat's flavor and texture like a carefully made BLT, so every effort should be made to acquire the most distinguished artisanal products available—no matter the cost. Also, when I make BLTs, this is one time I ignore the health risks and use home-made mayonnaise (otherwise, use only Hellmann's), and since nothing is worse than a soggy BLT (except in that lunch box), be sure to serve the sandwiches immediately—with, of course, potato chips.

6 thick slices applewood- or hickory-smoked bacon
4 slices top-quality white loaf bread
Mayonnaise
4 crisp leaves iceberg lettuce
4 slices ripe tomato
Salt and freshly ground black pepper to taste

• In a large skillet, fry the bacon over moderate heat till crisp and drain on paper towels.

• Lightly toast the bread slices and spread mayonnaise on one side of each slice while toast is still warm. Arrange 2 leaves of lettuce on the mayo side of 2 of the toast slices, top each with 2 slices of tomato, and season with salt and pepper. Arrange 3 slices of bacon over the tomatoes, place the remaining pieces of toast, mayo side down, on top of the bacon, slice the sandwiches on the diagonal, and secure each half with a frilly toothpick. Serve immediately.

MAKES 2 SANDWICHES

california stuffed hot dogs

Exactly who first prepared these succulent hot dogs now found in diners and family restaurants all over California remains a mystery, but I did hear or read somewhere that the actor/gastronome Vincent Price always prided himself on a version he served at his home. Do use the best-quality hot dogs (kosher ones are expensive but hard to beat), rolls, and cheese you can find, and nothing is better for these dogs than thin slices of lean, hickory-smoked commercial bacon, which browns fairly quickly.

2 tablespoons butter
2 medium onions, chopped
4 extra-long hot dogs
2 ounces Monterey Jack cheese, cut into strips
4 slices lean hickory-smoked bacon
Grainy mustard
4 hot dog rolls, lightly toasted and kept warm

• Preheat the oven broiler.

• In a skillet, melt the butter over moderate heat, add the onions, and stir till golden brown, about 10 minutes. Remove pan from the heat.

• Cut a deep slit lengthwise in each hot dog and fill each slit with equal amounts of onion. Place strips of cheese over the onions, wrap a bacon slice in a spiral around each hot dog, and secure with toothpicks soaked in water.

• Place the hot dogs on a rack in a baking pan and broil 5 inches from the heat, turning them often till the cheese melts and the bacon is browned. Remove the picks, spread mustard over the insides of the rolls, and stuff the hot dogs into the rolls. Serve the hot dogs hot with knives and forks.

MAKES 4 SERVINGS

swedish open-faced mussel and bacon sandwiches

Although Sweden is best known culinarily for its elaborate smorgasbords, some of the country's unusual open-faced sandwiches—laden with everything from pickled herring and onions to curried eggs to liver paste—match almost anything the Danes can come up with. Never could I imagine the affinity between fresh mussels and bacon till I had this delectable sandwich one day for lunch at a smart café in Malmö, and the fact that white toast was used instead of the more traditional sour rye or pumpernickel bread was fully justified by the way the residual juice of the mussels gradually seeped into the bread and contrasted with the crispy bacon. Since all Scandinavian bacon (whether Canadian- or streaky-style) tends to be very salty, the only seasoning needed, if you manage to find genuine Danish bacon, is a few grinds of pepper.

8 slices smoked Danish or slab bacon, rind removed
32 fresh mussels in the shell, scrubbed and bearded
2 tablespoons butter
4 large, thick, firm-textured slices white loaf bread, toasted
Freshly ground black pepper to taste
2 tablespoons chopped fresh dill

• In a large, heavy skillet, fry the bacon over moderate heat till almost crisp, drain on paper towels, and break crosswise in half. Pour off all but about 2 tablespoons of fat from the skillet and set the skillet aside.

• Place the mussels in a large pot and add about 2 inches of water. Bring the water to a boil, cover the pot, and steam the mussels about 2 minutes. Drain and, when cool enough to handle, shuck them, discarding any with shells that have not opened.

• Place the skillet back over moderate heat and add the butter to the bacon fat. Add the mussels and stir till slightly firm, 2 to 3 minutes. Divide the mussels evenly over the toasted bread slices, top each with equal pieces of bacon, season with black pepper, and sprinkle dill over the tops. Serve on sandwich plates with knives and forks.

MAKES 4 SERVINGS

casseroles
and stews

Virginia Brunswick Stew

Maytag Beef and Bacon Stew

Long Island Oyster and Bacon Casserole

Lima Bean and Bacon Casserole

Duck, Bacon, and Pinto Bean Stew

Sante Fe Venison Sausage and Canadian Bacon Stew

Key West Conch and Bacon Stew

Canadian Bacon, Corn, and Cheese Strata

Canadian Bacon, Sweet Potato, and Apple Casserole

Alsatian Baeckoffe

Italian Rabbit Stew

Spanish Chicken, Bacon, Meatball, and Chickpea Stew

Hungarian Venison and Bacon Ragout

Irish Hot Pot

Bahamian Lobster and Bacon Ragout

Japanese Braised Pork and Bacon with Chinese Cabbage

virginia brunswick stew

If Brunswick County, Virginia; Brunswick County, North Carolina; and Brunswick, Georgia, all lay heated claim to be the birthplace of Brunswick stew, you should hear the bickering among the respective stewmasters over the correct ingredients for the stew, the right cooking time and texture, the color, and even whether it must be served with cornbread, biscuits, or hush puppies. Being from North Carolina, with relatives in Virginia and Georgia, I backed out of the debate a long time ago and now just quietly go about concocting the same stew I've been serving crowds for years. What nobody questions, however, is the cardinal importance of some form of bacon in the stew: regular streaky or slab bacon, lean salt pork (or "streak-o'-lean"), or fatback. My one loud warning: nothing can stick and burn quicker than Brunswick stew, so be sure to stir it periodically while it's simmering, and constantly during the final 15 to 20 minutes as it thickens. Stored in individual containers, any leftover stew freezes well for future needs.

Two 3-pound chickens, cut up
8 ounces slab bacon or lean salt pork (rind removed), cut into cubes
4 pounds all-purpose potatoes
2½ pounds onions, chopped
8 tablespoons (1 stick) butter or margarine
3 tablespoons salt
3 tablespoons sugar
1½ teaspoons freshly ground black pepper
1½ teaspoons cayenne pepper
1½ quarts canned crushed tomatoes, juices included
2½ quarts small fresh or frozen lima beans
1½ quarts fresh or frozen corn kernels

• In a 12-quart cast-iron or heavy stainless-steel pot, combine the chicken and bacon and add enough water to cover by 1 inch. Bring to a boil, reduce the heat to a steady simmer, and cook, uncovered, till the chicken is very tender, about 1½ hours.

• Add the potatoes, onions, 2 tablespoons of the butter, 1 tablespoon each of salt and sugar, and pinches of black pepper and cayenne. Return to a simmer and cook till the potatoes are very tender, about 1 hour, stirring about every 15 minutes.

• Add the tomatoes plus their juices, another 2 tablespoons of the butter, 1 tablespoon each salt and sugar, and pinches of black pepper and cayenne. Return to a simmer and cook, stirring 10 minutes. Add the limas, another 2 tablespoons of the butter, and the remaining salt, sugar, black pepper, and cayenne. Return to a simmer and cook about 1 hour, stirring at least every 10 minutes.

• Add the corn and remaining 2 tablespoons of butter, return to a simmer, and cook, stirring constantly, till the stew is very thick, 15 to 20 minutes. Taste and, if necessary, adjust the seasoning. Ladle the stew into large soup bowls and serve piping hot.

MAKES AT LEAST 12 SERVINGS

BACON BONUS
A little finely chopped salty bacon or salt pork, or a teaspoon of bacon fat, added to sweet ingredients accentuates the sweetness of the food.

maytag beef and bacon stew

Newton, Iowa, is the home not only of Maytag washing machines but also of exceptional Maytag blue cheese, reason enough for me to visit the area some years ago and walk away with the recipe for this sumptuous stew included on a supper buffet I attended. Since then, I've experimented with different types of bacon for the dish and most recently have decided that nothing enhances the flavor better than a smoky artisanal peppered bacon. Do remember that the onions need to be stirred slowly over low heat to caramelize properly, and don't overdo the cheese.

5 slices lean peppered bacon
3 large onions, coarsely chopped
2 tablespoons vegetable oil
2½ pounds beef shoulder, trimmed of excess fat and cut into 1½-inch cubes
3 tablespoons all-purpose flour
1 cup ale or full-bodied beer
Pinch of dried thyme, crumbled
Pinch of dried rosemary, crumbled
2 bay leaves
Salt and freshly ground black pepper to taste
2 cups beef broth
1 tablespoon cider vinegar
1 cup crumbled Maytag blue cheese (available in most markets)

• In a large, heavy pot, fry the bacon over moderate heat till almost crisp, drain on paper towels, and crumble. Add the onions to the bacon fat, reduce the heat to very low, and cook them slowly, stirring, till nicely caramelized, about 20 minutes. Transfer the onions to a plate, add the vegetable oil to the remaining fat in the pot, and increase the heat to moderately high.

• On a large plate, dust the beef in the flour, tapping off any excess. Add to the pot and brown on all sides. Add the ale and stir, scraping any browned bits off the bottom of the pot. Add the crumbled bacon and onions to the pot and add the thyme, rosemary, bay leaves, salt and pepper, broth, and vinegar. Bring to a boil, reduce the heat to a simmer, cover, and cook till the beef is very tender, about 2 hours.

• Serve the stew in bowls with a little blue cheese sprinkled on top.

MAKES 4 SERVINGS

long island oyster and bacon casserole

On Long Island, where I live and where both Blue Point and Chincoteague oysters flourish in the many bays and inlets, natives learned long ago about the affinity of fresh oysters and wood-smoked bacon—in roasts, stews, and casseroles. For this basic casserole, I like the distinctive flavor of maple-smoked bacon, and to add a bit of mystery to the dish, I sometimes sprinkle about a tablespoon of dry sherry over the top before baking. The casserole can be served as either an appetizer for six or, with a platter of ham biscuits or sliced meats, a main course for three or four. And the casserole almost demands a sturdy dry white wine such as a Chablis.

6 slices lean maple-smoked bacon
1½ pints fresh, shucked oysters, liquor included
1½ cups half-and-half
2½ cups crumbled soda crackers
¾ cup (1½ sticks) butter, melted
Salt and freshly ground black pepper to taste
Tabasco sauce to taste

• Preheat the oven to 350°F. Butter a 1½-quart casserole and set aside.

• In a medium skillet, fry the bacon over moderate heat till almost crisp, drain on paper towels, and crumble.

• Drain the oysters, saving about ½ cup of the liquor. In a medium mixing bowl, combine the liquor and half-and-half, stir well, and set aside. In another medium mixing bowl, combine the cracker crumbs and butter, season with salt and pepper and Tabasco, and set aside.

• Sprinkle about a third of the cracker crumbs over the bottom of the prepared casserole, arrange half the oysters on top, sprinkle half the bacon over the oysters, and pour half the liquor mixture over the top. Add another third of the crumbs, arrange the remaining oysters on top, sprinkle on the remaining bacon, pour on the remaining liquor mixture, and top with the remaining crumbs. Bake till bubbly and lightly browned, about 35 minutes.

MAKES 6 APPETIZER SERVINGS OR 3 TO 4 MAIN-COURSE SERVINGS

lima bean and bacon casserole

I don't know which I love more, lima beans or bacon, and when you feature the two in a casserole with a little brown sugar, dry mustard, and tangy cheddar cheese, you simply can't serve a more delectable side dish. You could, of course, dice the bacon and combine it with the beans with tasty results, but I know of no better way to highlight a truly superior wood-smoked artisanal bacon than baking the strips on top till they're toothsomely crisp. It's not easy these days finding fresh, shelled summer limas (which I use when possible), but I must say the frozen (not canned) ones are almost as good.

Two 10-ounce packages frozen lima beans, cooked according to package directions, drained, with cooking liquid reserved
1 tablespoon solid butter plus 2 tablespoons melted
1 tablespoon all-purpose flour
1 tablespoon firmly packed light brown sugar
2 teaspoons dry mustard
2 teaspoons fresh lemon juice
Salt and freshly ground black pepper to taste
½ cup dry bread crumbs
½ cup shredded sharp cheddar cheese
6 slices lean applewood- or cob-smoked bacon

• Preheat the oven to 350°F. Butter a 1½-quart casserole and layer the drained beans over the bottom.

• In a small heavy saucepan, melt the 1 tablespoon butter over moderate heat, add the flour, and whisk for 1 minute. Slowly add ½ cup of the reserved cooking liquid from the beans, whisking till thickened and smooth. Add the brown sugar, mustard, and lemon juice, season with salt and pepper, stir till well blended, and pour over the limas.

• In a small mixing bowl, combine the bread crumbs, 2 tablespoons melted butter, and cheese, stir till well blended, and spoon the mixture evenly over the limas. Arrange the bacon slices over the top and bake till they are crisp, about 30 minutes.

MAKES 4 TO 6 SERVINGS

duck, bacon, and pinto bean stew

James Beard loved bacon like nobody I ever knew, and when I once brought him two fresh ducks from Long Island, he wasted no time transforming them into a luscious stew with pinto beans, small chunks of lean salt pork, and, of course, thin strips of fried cracklin's made from the duck skin. Since I like a smoky flavor to this stew, I now use an applewood- or hickory-smoked artisanal bacon, but whichever style of bacon you choose, just make sure it renders enough fat in which to brown the duck pieces.

2 cups dried pinto beans, picked over and rinsed
1 medium onion, peeled and stuck with 2 cloves, plus 2 medium onions, finely chopped
2 garlic cloves, peeled
1 bay leaf
Salt to taste
Two 4-pound ducks
5 tablespoons all-purpose flour
Freshly ground black pepper to taste
2 tablespoons butter
2 ounces fatty applewood- or hickory-smoked slab bacon (rind removed), diced
Pinch of dried basil, crumbled
½ teaspoon dry mustard
2 tablespoons vegetable oil

• Place the beans in a large saucepan with enough water to cover and let soak overnight.

• Drain the beans, add the clove-stuck onion, garlic, and bay leaf, and cover with salted water. Bring to a boil, reduce the heat to moderately low, and simmer for 30 minutes. Drain the beans, onion, and seasonings and reserve the cooking liquid.

• Skin and cut the ducks into serving pieces, removing as much fat as possible. Slice the skin into thin strips and set aside. On a plate, combine the flour and salt and pepper and dredge the duck pieces in the mixture, tapping off any excess flour. In a large, heavy skillet, heat the butter and bacon together over moderately high heat till the bacon renders most of its fat, then add the chopped onions and stir till softened, about 5 minutes. Transfer the bacon and onions to a large, heavy pot. In batches, brown the duck pieces evenly in the skillet and transfer to the pot. Add the beans plus their seasonings, the basil, mustard, and salt and pepper and stir. Add the reserved bean liquid plus, if necessary, enough water to cover. Bring to a simmer, cover, and cook till the duck and beans are very tender, about 2 hours.

• In a skillet, heat the oil over moderately high heat, add the reserved strips of duck skin, and fry till crisp. Drain the strips on paper towels and use to garnish the duck and beans.

MAKES 6 SERVINGS

sante fe venison sausage and canadian bacon stew

From western Texas to Utah and New Mexico, some of the best venison in the country is produced from deer that graze on the region's wild grasses, juniper, herbs, and piñon, and when spicy venison sausage (available in all local meat markets and delis, and many others nationwide) is simmered in beer with smoky Canadian bacon, various vegetables, and tart juniper berries, you're in for a very special stew. Five or six slices of lean streaky bacon can be substituted for the Canadian, in which case the peanut oil is unnecessary.

3 tablespoons peanut oil
4 to 5 medium slices Canadian bacon, cut into small dice
1½ pounds venison sausage links, cut into thirds
2 medium onions, chopped
1 garlic clove, minced
Two 12-ounce bottles beer
2 medium potatoes, peeled and cut into cubes
1 tablespoon juniper berries, crushed
1 teaspoon dried thyme, crumbled
2 bay leaves
Salt and freshly ground black pepper to taste
½ pound mushrooms, quartered
2 tablespoons all-purpose flour
2 tablespoons butter, softened
2 teaspoons prepared mustard

• In a large, heavy pot, heat 1 tablespoon of the oil over moderate heat, add the Canadian bacon, stir till lightly browned, and drain on paper towels. Add the remaining oil to the skillet, add the sausage, brown evenly on all sides, and transfer to a plate. Add the onions and garlic to the pot and stir till softened, about 5 minutes. Return the sausage to the pot and add the bacon, beer, potatoes, juniper berries, thyme, bay leaves, and salt and pepper. Bring to a low simmer, cover, and cook for 30 minutes. Add the mushrooms, stir, return to a simmer, and cook for 20 minutes. In a bowl, combine the flour, butter, and mustard, mixing well to form a paste. Stir the paste thoroughly into the stew to thicken and heat for 5 minutes.

MAKES 4 SERVINGS

key west conch and bacon stew

Used in most of coastal Florida and especially in Key West to make all types of delectable salads, fritters, chowders, and stews, the hideous-looking, tough mollusk known as conch (pronounced "conk") must first be pounded or finely chopped before its sweet meat is edible. During the summer you might find fresh conch in Chinese or Italian markets, but since it is highly perishable and lasts only a couple of days in the refrigerator, you're much better off buying the canned or frozen product. Natives of Key West learned long ago the affinity of conch and bacon, and while regular streaky bacon can certainly be used in this stew, a double-smoked artisanal one has much more flavor and stands up beautifully to the assertive conch. Don't snicker at the evaporated milk: in Key West it's a traditional ingredient in both conch stew and chowder.

4 slices double-smoked slab bacon, cut into small pieces
1 large onion, chopped
1 celery rib, chopped
1 garlic clove, minced
2 ripe medium tomatoes, chopped and juices retained
2 medium potatoes, peeled and cut into ½-inch cubes
2 pounds frozen conch meat, thawed, pounded till quite thin, and cut into 1-inch pieces
2 bay leaves
Salt and freshly ground black pepper to taste
2½ cups water
One 5-ounce can evaporated milk

• In a large, heavy pot, fry the bacon over moderate heat till almost crisp, then add the onion, celery, and garlic and cook, stirring, till soft, about 3 minutes. Add the tomatoes with their juices, potatoes, conch, bay leaves, salt and pepper, and water and bring to a boil. Reduce the heat to low, cover, and simmer till the conch is tender, about 1 hour. Pour in the evaporated milk and stir till the stew is heated through, never allowing it to boil. Serve hot in wide soup bowls.

MAKES 4 TO 6 SERVINGS

canadian bacon, corn, and cheese strata

In the South, a strata is any layered casserole that can be quickly assembled, covered, and left in the refrigerator till it's ready to be topped with buttered biscuit or bread crumbs and popped in the oven. For as long as I can remember, Canadian bacon has always been a major ingredient in this style of casserole, not only because of its distinctive smoky flavor but because the round slices lend themselves to easy layering. The assembled strata can be refrigerated overnight, but for the right texture, be sure to refrigerate it at least an hour before baking. This makes a great buffet dish.

16 medium slices good sourdough or multigrain bread
8 medium slices Canadian bacon
8 medium slices sharp cheddar cheese
2 cups fresh or frozen (and thawed) corn kernels
3 cups whole milk (not skim or low-fat)
6 large eggs, beaten
¼ cup minced scallions (white parts only)
¼ cup seeded and minced green bell pepper
1 teaspoon dry mustard
Salt and freshly ground black pepper to taste
Cayenne pepper to taste
1 cup dry bread crumbs
4 tablespoons (½ stick) butter, melted

• Trim any crusts from the bread and cut 8 of the bread slices to fit snugly in the bottom of a buttered 2-quart casserole. Top each slice with a piece of Canadian bacon, then a slice of cheese, and distribute the corn evenly over the top. Fit the remaining bread slices snugly over the corn.

• In a mixing bowl, combine the milk, eggs, scallions, bell pepper, and mustard, season with salt, black pepper, and cayenne pepper, and whisk till well blended. Pour the mixture over the casserole, cover with plastic wrap, and refrigerate overnight.

• Remove the casserole from the refrigerator 30 minutes before baking. Preheat the oven to 325°F.

• In a small mixing bowl, combine the bread crumbs and butter, mix well, spoon evenly over the casserole, and bake till browned on top, about 45 minutes. Serve hot.

MAKES 8 SERVINGS

canadian bacon, sweet potato, and apple casserole

Sweet potatoes, onions, and apples are a classic combination for any casserole, but when they are crowned with brown-sugar-glazed Canadian bacon slices that have been spread with a little zesty mustard, you have a dish fit for even the most stylish buffet. Since this casserole is so quick and easy to prepare (especially if the potatoes are boiled in advance), it's also perfect for a casual cool-weather supper, served with no more than a green salad and a loaf of country bread.

4 medium sweet potatoes, scrubbed
2 Granny Smith apples, peeled, cored, and cut into ¼-inch rounds
1 medium onion, chopped
Salt and freshly ground black pepper to taste
Dijon mustard
8 to 10 slices Canadian bacon, cut ¼ inch thick
2 tablespoons light brown sugar
3 tablespoons butter, cut into pieces

• Place the sweet potatoes in a pot with enough water to cover, bring to a boil, reduce the heat to moderate, and boil till barely tender, about 30 minutes. Drain and, when cool enough to handle, peel the potatoes and cut into ½-inch rounds.

• Preheat the oven to 375°F and butter a 2-quart casserole.

• Layer the potatoes and apples alternately in the casserole, sprinkle the onion over the top, and season with salt and pepper. Spread mustard lightly over each side of the bacon slices, then arrange the slices overlapping on top. Sprinkle the brown sugar over the top, dot with the butter, and bake till the bacon is nicely glazed, about 30 minutes. Serve hot.

MAKES 4 TO 5 SERVINGS

alsatian baeckoffe

Referring historically to the "baker's oven" where Alsatian housewives would leave their lusty stew in earthenware vessels to simmer slowly while doing the Monday morning wash, *baeckoffe* can include everything from various pork products to beef to all types of sausages and vegetables. In Alsace, the preferred bacon is either fresh unsmoked breast (*poitrine fraîche*) or smoked pork belly (*lard fumé*), both of which can often be ordered on specialty meat websites such as D'Artagnan. Otherwise, use a reliable artisanal slab bacon or, if necessary, ordinary lean slab bacon found in the supermarket. If you can't find a pig's foot, double the number of oxtails to ensure a sufficiently gelatinous texture to the stew. Traditionally, *baeckoffe* is served with a bowl of freshly grated horseradish and bottles of young Riesling.

1 pound lean slab bacon (rind removed)
1 pound boneless pork butt, trimmed of excess fat
1 pound boneless beef shoulder, trimmed of excess fat
1 pound oxtails
1 pound garlic sausage, thickly sliced
1 pig's foot
Herb bouquet (twigs of fresh parsley, thyme, and rosemary tied in cheesecloth)
2 medium leeks (white parts only), halved lengthwise and well rinsed
2 medium onions, chopped
Salt and freshly ground black pepper to taste
3½ cups Riesling wine
1 tablespoon red wine vinegar
5 medium red potatoes, sliced ¼ inch thick

• In a large stainless-steel or glass mixing bowl, combine all the meats. Add the herb bouquet, leeks, and onions, season with salt and pepper, and mix the ingredients with your hands. Add the wine, vinegar, and enough water to cover, cover with plastic wrap, and marinate in the refrigerator for 24 hours.

• Preheat the oven to 350°F.

• Layer half the potatoes in a 5-quart casserole, arrange the meats and vegetables on top, then layer the remaining potatoes. Pour the meat marinade over the top. Cover the casserole tightly and bake for 3½ hours.

• To serve, place helpings of potatoes in wide soup bowls; carve the meats on a carving board and distribute over the potatoes, then add more potatoes and a little broth to each bowl.

MAKES 6 TO 8 SERVINGS

italian rabbit stew

Known throughout northern Italy as *coniglio al Barolo*, even when it's not pre-pared with a noble Barolo wine, this rabbit stew depends as much on pancetta as on red wine for its succulent flavor. In Italy, most cooks have access to fresh rabbit in neighborhood butcher shops, but since many of our markets now carry excellent frozen rabbit that is dressed and cut up, there's really no need to go to the trouble of finding the fresh. Just make sure the rabbit is meaty and not too bony. A good substitute for expensive Barolo is either Barbera or a reliable California or Oregon Pinot Noir.

3 ounces pancetta, cut into small cubes
¼ cup olive oil
1 cup all-purpose flour
Salt and freshly ground black pepper to taste
3 pounds frozen cut-up rabbit, thawed
2 medium onions, chopped
½ green bell pepper, seeded and chopped
1 carrot, scraped and cut into small cubes
2 garlic cloves, minced
2 cups dry red wine
1 cup chopped Italian-style canned tomatoes, juices included
½ cup water
½ teaspoon dried rosemary
1 bay leaf

• In a 2- to 2½-quart casserole, lightly brown the pancetta over moderate heat, about 3 minutes, and transfer to a large bowl. Add 2 tablespoons of the olive oil to the casserole.

• On a large plate, combine the flour and salt and pepper, dredge the rabbit pieces in the mixture, shaking off the excess, then brown the pieces on all sides over moderate heat in the casserole, adding a little more oil if necessary. Transfer the pieces to the bowl with the pancetta.

• Add the remaining oil to the casserole, add the onions, bell pepper, carrot, and garlic, and stir till the vegetables soften, about 8 minutes. Add the vegetables to the bowl with the pancetta and rabbit.

• Add the wine to the casserole and stir, scraping the brown bits off the bottom. Add the pancetta, rabbit, and vegetables to the casserole, add the tomatoes, water, rosemary, bay leaf, and salt and pep-per to taste, and stir well. Bring to a boil, reduce the heat to low, cover, and simmer till the rabbit is fork-tender, about 1 hour.

MAKES 4 SERVINGS

spanish chicken, bacon, meatball, and chickpea stew

Every region of Spain has its hearty *cocido* (stew), concocted with everything from meaty bones and ground meats to exotic vegetables and beans to assorted bacons and sausages. In Madrid and the surrounding area, this particular stew would most likely be made with a cut of salt-cured hog belly known as *tocino,* our closest equivalent being salt pork with streaks of lean meat ("streak-o'-lean"). Dried chickpeas (garbanzos) can be found in all supermarkets and are superior to the canned ones, and today most meat markets and some delis carry chorizo sausage. Obviously, this stew is a full meal in itself, requiring nothing more than a chewy country bread and plenty of full-bodied Rioja wine.

1 cup dried chickpeas, soaked overnight
One 3-pound chicken, cut into serving pieces
½ pound streaky salt pork (or fatty slab bacon)
2 medium onions, sliced
2 medium leeks (white parts only), cut into thirds and rinsed well
2 carrots, scraped and cut into rounds
2 medium tomatoes, quartered
1 pound small red potatoes, peeled
1 chorizo sausage, cut into rounds
Salt and freshly ground black pepper to taste
½ pound ground beef chuck
1 large egg yolk
2 tablespoons bread crumbs
1 tablespoon chopped parsley leaves
2 tablespoons olive oil

• Place the chickpeas in a saucepan and add water to cover. Bring to a boil, reduce the heat to low, cover, and simmer till tender, about 2 hours.

• Place the chicken and bacon in a large pot, add water to cover by 1 inch, and bring to a boil. Reduce the heat to low, cover, and simmer 30 minutes. Add the onions, leeks, carrots, and tomatoes and continue simmering for 20 minutes. Add the potatoes and continue simmering for 20 minutes. Add the chickpeas, sausage, and salt and pepper and simmer about 15 minutes longer.

• Meanwhile, combine the ground beef, egg yolk, bread crumbs, parsley, and salt and pepper to taste in a bowl, mix till well blended, and shape the mixture into small meatballs. In a skillet, heat the oil over moderate heat, add the meatballs, and cook till browned all over, about 15 minutes. Add the meatballs to the stew and simmer the stew 10 minutes longer.

• With a slotted spoon, transfer the chicken pieces, bacon, and sausage to a large serving platter, remove and discard the bacon rind, and cut the bacon into slices. Strain the stock from the pot into a large bowl and serve it as soup in small soup bowls. Surround the meats with the chickpeas and vegetables and serve immediately.

MAKES 4 TO 6 SERVINGS

BACON BANTER
"Beans with bacon grease is always eaten from the pan with a tablespoon while standing over the kitchen sink. The pan must be thrown away immediately. The correct drink with this dish is a straight shot of room-temperature gin."
—RUSSELL BAKER

hungarian venison and bacon ragout

Back in the 1960s and '70s, the colorful Hungarian chef Louis Szathmáry caused a sensation in Chicago at his highly eclectic restaurant, The Bakery, and of all the amazing dishes I sampled there, none left such an impression as Chef Louis's succulent venison ragout enriched with heady paprika bacon (available today in most Hungarian or German markets and delis). If at all possible, use fresh beef stock (strained) for this ragout, and don't be jarred by the tomato juice and brown sugar: both are essential to the dish's success.

½ pound lean paprika bacon or slab bacon (rind removed), cut into ½-inch cubes
½ cup lard
3 scallions (white parts only), minced
1 garlic clove, minced
4 tablespoons all-purpose flour
1 teaspoon salt
1 teaspoon freshly ground black pepper
1 teaspoon sweet paprika
3 pounds boneless venison, cut into 1-inch cubes
1 cup dry red wine
1 teaspoon light brown sugar
½ cup tomato juice
1 cup beef broth
½ teaspoon dried thyme
1 tablespoon cornstarch
2 tablespoons butter
1 cup sliced fresh mushrooms
Boiled noodles or rice

• In a small saucepan, combine the bacon with 3 cups of water, bring to a boil, reduce the heat to low, and simmer 15 minutes. Drain the bacon and set aside.

• In a large pot, melt the lard over low heat, add the scallions and garlic, stir for 2 minutes, and remove from the heat.

• On a plate, combine 2 tablespoons of the flour, the salt, pepper, and paprika, and dredge the venison cubes in the mixture. Add the cubes to the scallions and garlic in the pot and brown the cubes on all sides over moderate heat, scraping the bottom of the pot with a spoon or spatula. Add ½ cup of the wine, the brown sugar, and the tomato juice, reduce the heat to low, cover, and cook 30 minutes, stirring occasionally.

(continued)

• Add the broth, thyme, bacon, and pepper to taste and increase the heat to moderate. Mix the remaining flour and the cornstarch into the remaining ½ cup of wine till smooth, add to the pot, and stir well for about 5 minutes. Reduce the heat to low, cover, and simmer the ragout for 1 hour.

• In a small skillet, melt the butter over moderate heat, add the mushrooms, and stir till golden, about 5 minutes. Add the mushrooms to the ragout and stir about 5 minutes longer. Serve the ragout hot over noodles or rice.

MAKES 6 TO 8 SERVINGS

irish hot pot

For an authentic hot pot, Irish cooks use what is called a "slipper joint" of smoked bacon, which is cut from the hog flank and most closely resembles our slab bacon. To retain enough fat to flavor the other ingredients slowly while simmering, the bacon is always initially boiled briefly, never fried, and it's rare to find a hot pot enhanced with either herbs or spices. What I love most about this hot pot are the buttery potatoes on top, which I'll often bake till they're crisp and almost slightly burnt. (Substitute a small head of roughly shredded cabbage leaves for the potatoes and you have what is considered to be almost the national dish of Ireland: braised cabbage and bacon.)

1½ pounds lean slab bacon (rind removed), cut into 1-inch cubes
5 carrots, scraped and sliced
3 medium onions, sliced
2 celery ribs, cut in half lengthwise and sliced
Salt and freshly ground black pepper to taste
1½ pounds red potatoes, peeled and sliced
Beef broth
2 tablespoons butter, melted
2 tablespoons chopped fresh parsley leaves

• Preheat the oven to 325°F.

• Place the bacon cubes in a saucepan and add enough water to cover. Bring slowly to a boil, then drain and set aside.

• In a bowl, combine the carrots, onions, celery, and salt and pepper and toss till well blended. Arrange a layer of potatoes in a 2-quart casserole, add a layer of bacon cubes, then a layer of vegetables. Continue making layers till all the ingredients are used up, ending with a layer of potatoes. Add enough broth to barely cover the ingredients, cover the casserole, and bake 1½ hours.

• Uncover, brush the top layer of potatoes with the melted butter, and continue baking till the broth has reduced slightly and the potatoes are golden brown, 15 to 20 minutes. Serve the stew sprinkled with parsley.

MAKES 4 TO 6 SERVINGS

bahamian lobster and bacon ragout

Spiny lobsters (or rock lobsters) are found all over the West Indies and differ from American (or Maine) lobsters in that they have no claws and almost all of the meat is in the tail. Also, since the meat is firmer and stringier than that of American lobsters, the spiny variety is ideal for all types of slow-simmering stews, ragouts, and casseroles. Spiny lobster tails are available frozen in many of our markets, but if you use them (cooked and shredded) for this ragout, remember that they need to be simmered with the bacon and vegetables up to 20 minutes, or till tender. More delicate (and sweeter) American lobsters, on the other hand, work just as well in this Bahamian specialty so long as they're not overcooked, which toughens the meat. Nothing more complex than ordinary streaky bacon is needed for this dish.

Three 1-pound live lobsters
4 thick slices streaky bacon, diced
1 medium onion, chopped
1 celery rib, chopped
½ medium green bell pepper, seeded and chopped
¼ cup tomato paste
4 large ripe tomatoes, peeled, seeded, and diced, with juices included
½ teaspoon fresh thyme leaves
1 small jalapeño pepper, finely chopped
Salt and freshly ground black pepper to taste
1 tablespoon water
Boiled long-grain white rice

• In a large stockpot, bring about 8 inches of water to a rolling boil and plunge the lobsters head-first into the water. Reduce the heat to low, cover, and steam the lobsters about 7 minutes. Remove from the water with tongs, crack the shells with a mallet or hammer, and, when cool enough to handle, shred the lobster meat and set aside.

• In a large skillet, fry the bacon over moderate heat just till it renders most of its fat, add the onion, celery, and bell pepper, and stir about 5 minutes. Add the lobster meat, tomato paste, tomatoes, thyme, jalapeño, and salt and pepper and stir till the mixture is soft, 8 to 10 minutes. Add the water and stir about 3 minutes longer.

• Serve the ragout hot over mounds of rice.

MAKES 6 SERVINGS

japanese braised pork and bacon with chinese cabbage

For this layered Japanese casserole, the pork slices should be as thin as you can slice them. The best results, of course, are produced on an electric meat slicer, but given that impracticality, one helpful trick is to partially freeze the loin before slicing it with a very sharp knife. If Chinese cabbage is unavailable, use either Savoy cabbage or heads of Belgian endive. As for the bacon, it should have sufficient fat to be released slowly during the cooking process, giving the casserole a silky texture.

½ pound boneless pork loin, thinly sliced
1 garlic clove, minced
1 teaspoon grated fresh ginger plus 1 tablespoon chopped
1 tablespoon soy sauce
1 tablespoon sake
One 1-pound head Chinese cabbage, leaves separated and discolored ones discarded
1 carrot, scraped and cut into 2-inch strips
½ pound lean streaky bacon slices, cut in half
1¼ cups chicken broth
2 teaspoons cornstarch mixed with 1 tablespoon water
Freshly ground black pepper to taste
Boiled rice

• Place the pork slices in a shallow pan or dish. In a small bowl, combine the garlic, grated ginger, soy sauce, and sake, stir till well blended, pour over the pork, and let marinate about 30 minutes.

• Divide the cabbage leaves and carrot strips into 4 portions, then divide the pork, bacon, and chopped ginger into 3 portions. Arrange one portion of leaves and strips on the bottom of a large pot, then cover with a portion of the meats and chopped ginger. Continue layering the ingredients in like manner, ending with a layer of leaves and strips. Add the broth, bring to a low boil, reduce the heat to moderate, cover, and cook till the meats are tender, about 20 minutes.

• Reduce the heat to low, add the cornstarch mixture and pepper, stir gently, and continue cooking till the broth thickens, about 2 minutes. Serve the hot meats, vegetables, and broth over mounds of rice.

MAKES 4 SERVINGS

main
courses

Chinese Lion's Head
Japanese Braised Pork Belly
Braised Veal Kidneys with Bacon and Wild Mushrooms
Chicken, Onions, and Bacon Braised in Zinfandel
Southern-Style Smothered Chicken with
Bacon and Lemon Slices
Italian Roasted Turkey Breast Stuffed with
Pancetta, Raisins, and Pine Nuts
Chicken and Bacon Succotash
French Squabs with Bacon and Mushroom Sauce
English Roast Guinea Hens with Bacon and Mushrooms
Bacon-Wrapped Roasted Quail Stuffed with Oysters
Baked Marinated Quail
Belgium Braised Rabbit, Prunes, and Bacon in Beer
New England Clam Hash
Louisiana Shrimp Creole
Baked Oysters with Mustard Greens and Bacon
Norwegian Bacon-Wrapped Broiled Salmon
Canadian Salmon, Potato, and Bacon Torte
Basque Salt Cod with Bacon and Tomatoes

italian braised beef and onions with pancetta

Leave it to Italian cooks to moisten an otherwise dry beef roast and infiltrate it with spicy flavor by larding the meat with strips of pancetta. Also, the slow braising allows the copious amount of onions to provide much of the necessary liquid, making this probably the easiest and most delicious roast beef you'll ever prepare. A beef shoulder roast or even a flat-cut brisket can be substituted for the top round with equally succulent results.

¼ pound whole pancetta
One 2-pound boneless top round beef roast
Salt and freshly ground black pepper to taste
2 large Spanish onions, thinly sliced
1 cup dry red wine

- Preheat the oven to 300°F.
- Cut half the pancetta into ¼-inch-wide strips and the other half into large dice, reserving the diced part. Using a larding needle or similar blunt utensil or stick, lard the roast by pushing the pancetta strips into the meat at various points. Season the roast with salt and pepper.
- In a heavy 2-quart casserole, layer the onion slices across the bottom, sprinkle the diced pancetta over the onions, and add the wine. Place the roast on top, cover tightly, and braise in the oven till the meat is very tender when tested with a small knife, about 3 hours, turning the roast twice.
- To serve, place the roast on a surface, carve in medium-thin slices, and arrange the slices on a serving platter. Pour the onions, pancetta, and sauce over the meat and serve immediately.

MAKES 4 TO 6 SERVINGS

german beef and bacon rolls

Rouladen are one of the staples of classic German cooking, and whether I'm in Berlin, Munich, or Baden-Baden, I go out of my way to find restaurants and colorful *Stuben* that serve the succulent meat rolls. Always accompanied by the pasta known as *Spaetzle,* the rolls must be made with German *Speck* or double-smoked bacon to have authentic flavor, and strange as it may sound, no chef would dream of preparing *Rouladen* without the obligatory strips of dill pickle.

1½ pounds top round beef, cut into 4-by-11-inch slices
Salt and freshly ground black pepper to taste
2 teaspoons dried marjoram
Grainy mustard
¼ pound German *Speck* or double-smoked slab bacon (rind removed), cut into ¼-inch cubes
1 large onion, finely chopped
¼ cup finely chopped parsley leaves
¼ cup finely chopped fresh chives
Six ½-inch strips dill pickle
4 tablespoons (½ stick) butter
1 carrot, scraped and thinly sliced
½ cup beef broth
½ cup dry red wine
½ teaspoon all-purpose flour
1 teaspoon water
½ cup heavy cream

• Sprinkle one side of the beef slices with salt and pepper and marjoram and spread mustard all over the tops. In a bowl, combine 1 cup of the bacon cubes with half the chopped onion, the parsley, and the chives, toss, and spread equal amounts of the mixture over each beef slice to within ½ inch of the edges. Place a pickle strip over the top of each slice, roll up the slices snugly, and secure each roll with a metal skewer.

• In a saucepan, melt 1 tablespoon of the butter over moderate heat, add the carrot slices and remaining onions and bacon, stir till the vegetables are lightly browned, about 10 minutes, and set aside.

• In a large, heavy skillet, melt the remaining 3 tablespoons butter over moderate heat, add the meat rolls, brown on all sides, and transfer to a plate. Add the broth and wine to the skillet and stir, scraping up the brown particles. In a bowl, blend the flour and water, add to the skillet, and stir till well blended. Return the meat rolls and bacon mixture to the skillet, cover, reduce the heat slightly, and cook for 1 hour, turning the rolls once.

• Transfer the rolls to a plate, spoon the sauce into a blender or food processor, blend till smooth, and return the sauce to the skillet. Add the cream, stir, and bring to a boil. Return the meat rolls to the skillet, cover, and simmer 10 to 15 minutes. Serve hot.

MAKES 6 SERVINGS

BACON BONUS
After discarding any stored bacon fat that has turned rancid, be sure to wash and dry the container to prevent rancid residue that would ruin fresh fat.

jean's best meat loaf

When I noticed in her cookbook *Quick Loaves* that my friend Jean Anderson had provided a recipe for her grandmother's meat loaf that included not only bacon inside and outside the loaf but also a little baking powder for lightness, I couldn't make the dish fast enough. Like her grandma, however, I did use regular whole milk for soaking the bread crumbs instead of the fat-free evaporated milk Jean calls for, as well as an ordinary yellow onion in place of chopped scallions. Suffice it to say that, even with my slight modifications, the result is one of the most flavorful, moist, glorious meat loaves ever conceived—thanks mostly to all the bacon.

3 cups soft white bread crumbs
1 cup whole milk
7 slices lean streaky bacon
1½ pounds lean ground beef (preferably a mixture of chuck and round)
1 medium onion, chopped
1 small green bell pepper, cored, seeded, and chopped
1 celery rib, chopped
½ cup ketchup
½ teaspoon baking powder
½ teaspoon freshly ground black pepper

- Preheat the oven to 350°F. Grease a 9-by-5-by-3-inch loaf pan and set aside.
- Place the bread crumbs in a large mixing bowl, drizzle the milk over the top, and let soak. Meanwhile, fry 2 slices of the bacon in a small skillet over moderate heat till crisp, drain on paper towels, and crumble finely.
- Add the crumbled bacon plus all remaining ingredients except the 5 remaining bacon slices to the soaked bread crumbs and mix with your hands till thoroughly blended. Transfer the mixture to the prepared pan, mounding slightly in the center, and bake for 20 minutes. Remove from the oven, increase the heat to 375°F, and arrange the 5 remaining bacon slices lengthwise on top of the loaf, overlapping slightly and tucking the ends down against the pan with a spatula.
- Return the loaf to the oven and bake till the bacon is nicely browned, 35 to 40 minutes. Cool the loaf in the pan about 20 minutes, pouring off the fat, then transfer to a plate and cut into slices.

MAKES 6 TO 8 SERVINGS

caribbean beef-and-bacon-stuffed plantains

A starchy banana-shaped fruit found throughout the Caribbean, the plantain tastes a little like a yam when cooked and is used by natives in as many different ways as we do potatoes. Now much more widely available in our markets, fully ripe, black-skinned plantains are generally baked or sautéed in bacon fat or butter, but those intended to be stuffed and deep-fried, as in this delectable specialty of the island of Barbados, should be still partly green with black spots over the surface—firm enough to hold their shape when sliced. These small packets are commonly served as a main course with some form of rice on the side. The plantains can be tricky to stuff; just make sure the stuffing is tightly packed in the plantain strips before deep-frying.

8 slices streaky bacon
3 semi-ripe plantains, peeled
¾ pound ground beef round
2 medium onions, finely chopped
2 ripe medium tomatoes, chopped
1 small green bell pepper, seeded and finely chopped
2 garlic cloves, minced
½ teaspoon dried thyme
Salt and freshly ground black pepper to taste
Peanut oil, for deep-frying
2 large eggs, beaten

• In a large, heavy skillet, fry the bacon over moderate heat till almost crisp, drain on paper towels, and crumble. Slice each plantain lengthwise into 4 strips, fry the strips in the bacon fat till just golden, about 10 minutes, and drain on paper towels. When cool enough to handle, shape each strip into a circle, secure with toothpicks, and set aside.

• Brown the beef in the remaining fat, breaking it up, add the onions, tomatoes, bell pepper, garlic, thyme, crumbled bacon, and salt and pepper, and cook, stirring from time to time, till the vegetables are softened, about 15 minutes. Fill each plantain circle compactly with equal amounts of the stuffing and secure the edges as tightly as possible.

• Heat about 2 inches of oil in the skillet to 375°F on a deep-frying thermometer, dip the stuffed plantains into the eggs, and fry 2 minutes. Carefully turn the plantains over with a spatula and fork, fry till golden brown, 2 to 3 minutes, and drain briefly on paper towels. Serve hot.

MAKES 4 TO 6 SERVINGS

canadian meat pie

Often considered the signature dish of Quebec, *tourtière* is a rustic specialty that has as many ingredient variations as cooking techniques. Some chefs might add chicken, rabbit, or wild game, but no matter how creative they become, none would make the pie without including pork in the form of both loin or shoulder and, of course, the lean peameal or back bacon that is world renowned. This is a sturdy cold-weather dish intended to be served with a tart salad or crispy vegetables and plenty of red wine or dark ale.

FOR THE DOUGH
1¼ cups all-purpose flour
6 tablespoons (¾ stick) cold butter, cut into bits
2 tablespoons cold lard, cut into bits
¼ teaspoon salt
3 tablespoons ice water

FOR THE PIE
3 tablespoons lard
3 thick slices Canadian peameal or back bacon, cut into pieces
1 pound lean pork, cut into 1-inch cubes
1 onion, chopped
1 garlic clove, minced
½ teaspoon salt
Freshly ground black pepper to taste
¼ teaspoon ground nutmeg
¼ teaspoon ground cloves
¼ teaspoon celery seed
1½ teaspoons cornstarch
1 cup water
1 cup cubed boiled potatoes

• To make the dough, combine the flour, butter, lard, and salt in a mixing bowl and blend with your fingertips till the mixture is mealy. Add the water, stir well, and form the dough into a ball. Place on a lightly floured surface and knead about 30 seconds. Reform into a ball, dust with flour, wrap in plastic wrap, and chill for 1 hour.

• Meanwhile, to make the pie, melt the lard in a large, heavy saucepan, add the bacon, and stir for 2 minutes. Add the pork, onion, and garlic and cook with the bacon for 3 minutes, stirring. Add the seasonings, cornstarch, and water, bring liquid to a boil, reduce the heat, cover, and simmer for 30 minutes. Uncover, add the potatoes, and cook for 5 minutes longer.

• Preheat the oven to 425°F. Grease a 9-inch pie pan and set aside.

• Divide the chilled dough in half and, on a lightly floured surface, roll out each half about ⅛ inch thick. Line the prepared pan with half the dough, scrape the pork and potato mixture into the pan, and cover with the remaining dough. Press the edges of the pie together and prick the top with a fork. Bake for 10 minutes, reduce the heat to 350°F, and bake till golden, about 30 minutes. Serve hot in wedges.

MAKES 4 TO 6 SERVINGS

BACON BONUS
A fine artisanal smoked bacon is best cut thick and broiled; a medium-thick one lends itself well to frying over moderate heat or baking at 350°F till not too crisp or too limp; and any paper-thin bacon should be slowly broiled till just barely crisp and not in the least burnt.

hungarian stuffed pork cutlets

Gundel is by far the best and most sophisticated restaurant in Budapest, and of all the Hungarian specialties I've sampled there, none has impressed me more than the highly original stuffed pork cutlets "sewn" together with thin strips of bacon. Ideally, a larding needle should be used for the unusual procedure, but since it's the dickens trying to thread the bacon through the eye of a needle, as the chefs at the restaurant do so deftly, I've modified the technique by simply cutting small slits in the edges of the cutlets and carefully threading the bacon through the slits to seal the packets as tightly as possible. If you can find Hungarian paprika bacon, by all means use it; if not, a good double-smoked one is just as effective. Remember that these cutlets need to be at once nicely browned and still moist.

8 boneless pork cutlets (about 1¼ pounds)
3 tablespoons lard
1 medium onion, minced
¼ pound ground lean pork
¼ pound ground pork liver
½ cup water
¼ cup cooked rice
1 large egg, beaten
Salt and freshly ground black pepper to taste
6 thin slices double-smoked bacon, cut lengthwise into thin strips

• With a mallet, pound the pork cutlets about ¼ inch thick (or slightly less) and set aside on a platter.

• In a medium skillet, heat 1 tablespoon of the lard over low heat, add the onion, and stir till wilted, about 10 minutes. Add the ground pork and pork liver, mix well, and cook, stirring, about 2 minutes. Add 1 tablespoon of the water, cover, and cook 30 minutes, stirring from time to time. Add the rice, egg, and salt and pepper and continue stirring till the stuffing is well blended and nicely bound.

• Place 4 of the pounded cutlets on a work surface and spoon equal amounts of stuffing in the center of each. Cover with the remaining 4 cutlets, press the edges firmly together, then, cutting small slits through the edges with a sharp paring knife, thread the edges of the packets with strips of bacon.

• In a large skillet, melt the remaining 2 tablespoons lard over moderately high heat and lightly brown the packets on both sides. Add the remaining water to the skillet and continue cooking till the liquid evaporates and the packets are nicely browned on both sides, about 10 minutes, turning once. Serve hot.

MAKES 4 SERVINGS

serbian stuffed cabbage leaves

I've known ardent bacon lovers in my day, but none so passionate as a native Serbian friend in Chicago whose preferred way of eating a double-smoked *Speck* or gypsy bacon is raw—as a snack. There's not much that Jovan can't do with a half pound of good bacon, but I think his masterpiece is these stuffed cabbage leaves that are traditionally served in Serbia and along the Dalmatian coast on Christmas Eve. The stuffing can be "tightened" with boiled rice and flavored with even more spices; the packages can be baked covered with sauerkraut; and it would be unheard of to serve the dish without a few boiled parsleyed potatoes.

18 large green cabbage leaves, white stems trimmed
2 medium onions, finely chopped
¼ cup finely chopped fresh parsley leaves
2 garlic cloves, minced
½ pound young spinach, rinsed, dried, and shredded
1 pound bulk pork sausage
½ pound lean ground pork
¼ cups all-purpose flour
2 large eggs, beaten
¼ teaspoon sweet paprika
Pinch of ground cinnamon
Pinch of ground nutmeg
Salt and freshly ground black pepper to taste
12 slices double-smoked bacon
2½ cups chicken broth

- In a large pot of boiling water, blanch the cabbage leaves for 2 minutes and drain on paper towels.
- Preheat the oven to 350°F.
- In a large bowl, combine the onions, parsley, garlic, and spinach and mix well. Add the sausage, pork, flour, eggs, paprika, cinnamon, nutmeg, and salt and pepper and mix with your hands till well blended. Divide the mixture into 6 equal portions.
- Arrange the cabbage leaves in 6 piles of 3 leaves each and place a portion of sausage mixture on each pile. Fold each pile into a package, wrap each snugly with 2 slices of bacon, and secure with skewers or heavy toothpicks. Arrange the packages in a medium baking dish or casserole, add the broth, cover, and bake 1½ hours. Serve hot with a little of the cooking liquid spooned over the top.

MAKES 6 SERVINGS

philippine adobo

Prepared with pork, chicken, seafood, or vegetables, plus some form of bacon, adobo is the national dish of the Philippines and a delightful buffet item served with a variety of exotic fruits and a spicy wine. The vinegar, which was originally used to preserve meats and poultry, is the key ingredient that gives the dish its distinctive taste, and in the Philippines, it's not unusual for some cooks to tame the final broth with a little coconut milk. Although many adobos are traditionally made with plain, unsmoked pork belly, I think a lightly smoked slab bacon (and its grease) adds lots more flavor. One more bit of advice: the adobo is best when chilled overnight and served the next day.

2 pounds pork shoulder, trimmed of excess fat and cut into 1½-inch pieces
10 garlic cloves, peeled and crushed
1 teaspoon black peppercorns, crushed
1 bay leaf
½ cup cider vinegar
2 tablespoons soy sauce
2 cups water
½ pound slab bacon (rind removed), cut into 1-inch pieces
Cooked long-grain rice

• In a large bowl, combine the pork, garlic, peppercorns, bay leaf, vinegar, and soy sauce, toss well, cover with plastic wrap, and refrigerate overnight.

• In a large stainless-steel or enameled pot, combine the pork mixture and water, bring to a boil, reduce the heat to low, cover, and simmer for 1 hour. Uncover, increase the heat to moderate, and continue cooking till the pork is tender and the broth is reduced to about 1½ cups, about 30 minutes. Strain the broth into a small bowl, transfer the pork mixture to a large bowl, discard the bay leaf, and set aside.

• In the same pot, fry the bacon over moderate heat till almost crisp and transfer to a plate. Pick out the pork pieces from the pork mixture and brown them evenly in the bacon fat. Add the garlic, peppercorns, and bacon and stir till the garlic is lightly browned and some of it has turned into a paste, about 2 minutes. Add the strained broth, reduce the heat to low, and simmer about 5 minutes.

• Mound hot rice on serving plates and spoon equal amounts of adobo over the mounds.

MAKES 4 SERVINGS

brazilian feijoada

The national dish of Brazil, *feijoada* involves not only black beans and large hunks of meat, sausage, bacon, and even pig's feet, ears, tail, and tongue, but also several days of preparation. Served with rice, shredded boiled kale, hearts of palm, orange slices, hot peppers, and cornbread, it's a culinary festivity, to be sure. Although I've streamlined the dish with readily available pork products and simplified the cooking technique, my version has never failed to please a crowd. Serve the *feijoada* with any of the side items mentioned above, plus plenty of ice-cold beer.

1 pound dried black beans
6 cups water
1 pound boneless ham, cut into ½-inch cubes
1 pound boneless pork loin, cut into ½-inch cubes
1 pound lean double-smoked slab bacon (rind removed), cut into ½-inch cubes
½ pound hot Italian sausage, cut into 1-inch rounds
1 large onion, chopped
1 pint cherry tomatoes
6 garlic cloves, minced
1 teaspoon red pepper flakes
¼ teaspoon grated orange rind

- Place the beans in a bowl with enough cold water to cover and let soak overnight.
- Preheat the oven to 350°F.
- In a 4- to 5-quart Dutch oven, combine the beans, 6 cups of water, and all remaining ingredients and stir well. Bring to a boil, skimming any scum from the surface. Cover, transfer to the oven, and bake 1½ hours. Uncover and bake till the meats are fork tender, about 30 minutes longer, stirring from time to time. Serve hot.

MAKES AT LEAST 10 SERVINGS

french bacon, ham, and prune pie

A specialty of France's Auvergne province rarely found outside the region, *pounti* is traditionally served as a main course, accompanied by a big pot of the luscious potato, cheese, and garlic purée known as *aligot*. Some home cooks make the dish with Swiss chard, others with spinach, or, around the town of Aurillac, with beet greens, but the essential ingredients in any *pounti* is the cured pork belly streaked with lean called *ventrèche* (available online from D'Artagnan and other imported-meat specialists). This particular version was inspired by a long talk I had with an elderly lady in Saint-Flour at the amazing food shop Aux Produits d'Auvergne.

10 pitted prunes
2 teaspoons active dry yeast
¼ cup warm water
1½ cups minced *ventrèche* bacon or lean salt pork with rind removed
1 cup minced cooked ham
2 medium onions, minced
½ cup minced Swiss chard or spinach leaves
1½ teaspoons chopped fresh chervil, or ½ teaspoon dried
1½ teaspoons chopped fresh tarragon, or ½ teaspoon dried
⅔ cup all-purpose flour
1 cup milk
4 large eggs, beaten
Salt and freshly ground black pepper to taste
3 tablespoons butter

• Place the prunes in a saucepan with enough water to cover, bring to a boil, reduce the heat to low, and simmer gently 30 minutes. Remove from the heat, cover, let stand for 15 minutes, and drain.

• In a small bowl, combine the yeast and water, stir, and let proof for 10 minutes.

• Preheat the oven to 350°F.

• In a large bowl, combine the bacon, ham, onion, Swiss chard, chervil, tarragon, and flour and stir well. Whisk in the milk and eggs, add the prunes, yeast mixture, and salt and pepper, and stir well. Rub the sides and bottom of a large, deep ovenproof skillet with the butter, heat the skillet over moderately high heat about 2 minutes, pour in the batter, and cook for 1 minute. Transfer the skillet to the oven and bake the pie till golden brown, about 40 minutes.

• To serve, loosen the pie with a spatula, transfer to a heated platter, and cut into 4 wedges. (The pie is also good served at room temperature.)

MAKES 4 SERVINGS

swiss potato and bacon cake

The quintessential Swiss-German dish, *rösti* potatoes are generally no more than grated potatoes pan-fried in butter as a cake till golden and crusty and served traditionally with diced veal in a creamy mushroom sauce. In and around the cheese town of Appenzell, however, chefs transform the simple side dish into a sturdy main course by adding smoky home-cured bacon to the cake and melting the assertive, tangy local cheese over the top. In a word, it's one of the most glorious creations I've ever tasted—perfect for a casual supper with no more than a salad and bottle of red Swiss Dôle.

Do try to find genuine German Black Forest bacon for this dish, but since Appenzeller cheese is brutally expensive in our markets (and often not in the best of shape), feel free to substitute either Swiss Gruyère or Vacherin. What is essential is to use only waxy, low-starch potatoes such as round whites or reds, as well as a heavy, preferably nonstick skillet.

5 medium red potatoes (about 2½ pounds), unpeeled
Salt and freshly ground black pepper to taste
3½ ounces Black Forest or lean slab bacon (rind removed), cut into small cubes
2 tablespoons butter, or more
5 ounces Appenzeller or Gruyère cheese, grated

• In a large pot, combine the potatoes with enough water to cover, bring to a boil, reduce the heat to moderate, and cook till just slightly softened, about 15 minutes. Drain, let cool, and chill the potatoes at least 3 hours or overnight.

• Peel and grate the potatoes on a coarse cheese grater into a large bowl. Season with salt and pepper and toss well.

• In a large, heavy skillet, fry the bacon over moderate heat till the fat runs and add 1 tablespoon of the butter. Add the potatoes, mix well, and, with a heavy spatula, press them down to form a cake. Cook till the underside is golden and crusty, about 20 minutes, then transfer the cake to a plate. Add the remaining butter plus more, if desired, to the skillet, slide the cake back in on the other side, and cook about 10 minutes. Sprinkle the grated cheese evenly over the top, cover, and let cook 5 to 10 minutes or till the cheese has melted. Cut the cake into individual portions and serve immediately.

MAKES 3 TO 4 SERVINGS

chinese lion's head

This popular Cantonese dish with the exotic, mysterious name is one of the most delectable ways I've learned to demonstrate the subtle spiciness of Chinese bacon (available air-dried in most Chinese markets). Just remember that since the bacon is most likely hard, it must be soaked in water (preferably overnight) before it can be diced. If it's impossible to find Chinese bacon, the closest substitute is pancetta. Like so many Chinese dishes, this one is intended to be shared on a communal basis with any number of other dishes.

2 pounds air-cured green Chinese or regular cabbage, leaves separated and rinsed
1½ pounds Chinese bacon, soaked in water overnight and rind removed
1 cup crushed soda crackers
6 tablespoons water
3 tablespoons dry sherry
2 tablespoons soy sauce
1 tablespoon cornstarch
Salt to taste
2 scallions (part of green leaves included), finely chopped
1 large egg
Peanut oil, for deep frying
1 tablespoon sugar

• Reserve 4 whole leaves of cabbage, chop the remaining leaves into bite-size pieces, and set aside.

• With a cleaver or large chef's knife, cut the bacon into small dice and place in a mixing bowl. Add the crushed crackers and blend the mixture with your hands. Add the water, 1 tablespoon each of the sherry and soy sauce, the cornstarch, and salt and mix till well blended. Add the scallions and mix till well blended. Shape equal amounts of the mixture into 4 balls and flatten each to about 4 inches in diameter. In a bowl, beat the egg, then coat each ball all over with egg.

• In a wok or deep skillet, heat about ½ inch of oil till very hot but not smoking and fry each ball about 30 seconds, basting the tops with hot oil till browned. Drain the balls on paper towels and pour off all but 3 tablespoons of oil from the pan.

• Add the chopped cabbage to the 3 tablespoons of oil in the pan and stir-fry for 1 minute. Add the remaining sherry and soy sauce, plus the sugar, and stir the cabbage about 3 minutes longer, adding a little water if the cabbage seems too dry.

• Cover the bottom of a 3-quart flameproof casserole with the chopped cabbage and spoon the juices over the top. Arrange the meatballs over the cabbage, sprinkling 2 or 3 tablespoons of water over the top. Cover the casserole and cook over moderate heat for 1 hour.

• To serve, spoon the cabbage onto a deep serving platter, cut the meatballs in half, and place the halves on top of the cabbage. Serve hot.

MAKES 6 TO 8 SERVINGS

japanese braised pork belly

Pork belly, which is generally uncured, unsmoked bacon much like Spain's *tocino* and Portugal's *toucinho,* has been prized in Japan for centuries and can be delicious when fried, grilled, or slowly braised with vegetables and the flavorful soybean paste known as miso. Since part of the fat in this recipe is rendered during the long simmering and later discarded after the belly has chilled overnight, the meat is actually quite firm when finally served in an aromatic broth—usually with plenty of boiled rice on the side. Pork belly is available from Niman Ranch and other websites, and you can find miso (in different colors and stages of aging) in all Asian markets and many specialty food shops.

8 cups water
1 small onion, cut in half
1 small carrot, scraped and cut in half, plus 1 carrot scraped and minced
1 garlic clove, cut in half
One 2-inch piece fresh ginger, cut in half
½ cup red miso
2 teaspoons sugar
2 pounds pork belly
Salt and freshly ground black pepper to taste
2 tablespoons peanut oil
2 scallions (part of green leaves included), chopped

• In a large pot, combine the water, onion, carrot halves, garlic, ginger, miso, and sugar. Bring to a boil, reduce the heat to low, and let simmer.

• Meanwhile, cut the pork belly in half, trim the outer layer of fat to about ½ inch, season with salt and pepper, and tie each half snugly with kitchen twine. In a large skillet, heat the oil over moderately high heat, add the pork, and brown on all sides, about 8 minutes in all.

• Return the broth in the pot to a boil and lower the pork bundles into the liquid. Reduce the heat to low, cover, and braise slowly till the pork is tender, 2½ to 3 hours. Let cool completely, cover the pot, and refrigerate overnight.

• Discard the fat that has risen to the top, transfer the pork to a work surface, remove the twine, and cut the meat into 1½-inch cubes. Strain the broth into another pot, discard the vegetables, add the meat to the broth, and bring to a simmer. Serve the hot pork and broth in shallow bowls with chopped scallions and minced carrots sprinkled over the top.

MAKES 4 SERVINGS

braised veal kidneys with bacon and wild mushrooms

Of all the variety meats now available in most markets, veal kidneys remain one of the most delicate and prized, and when they're braised with a superior bacon and exotic mushrooms, the result is delectable. For my taste, hickory- or cob-smoked bacon best complements the kidneys, but do feel free to experiment. Likewise, virtually any wild mushroom can be used. If you prefer more pungent flavor, lamb kidneys can be substituted for the veal so long as they're first soaked about one hour in milk, the cores removed, and the membranes trimmed. I like these kidneys served over boiled white long-grain or wild rice.

2 pounds veal kidneys, any membranes and hard cores removed
3 thick, lean slices hickory- or cob-smoked bacon, cut into small dice
1 medium onion, finely chopped
½ cup all-purpose flour
Salt and freshly ground black pepper to taste
2 cups beef broth
½ pound wild mushrooms (cèpes, chanterelles, or morels), stems removed and caps quartered
¼ teaspoon dried rosemary, crumbled
1 bay leaf, crumbled
1 tablespoon all-purpose flour mixed with 1 tablespoon water
1 tablespoon minced fresh parsley leaves

• Place the kidneys in a bowl, add enough water to cover, and soak about 30 minutes at room temperature. Meanwhile, in a large, heavy pot, fry the bacon over moderate heat till almost crisp, add the onion, stir about 2 minutes, and set the pot aside.

• Drain the kidneys, pat dry with paper towels, and cut into 1-inch cubes. On a plate, combine the flour and salt and pepper and dredge the kidneys in the mixture, tapping off any excess flour. Add the kidneys to the pot and brown over moderate heat, stirring. Add the broth, mushrooms, rosemary, and bay leaf, bring to a moderate simmer, scraping any browned bits off the bottom, cover, and cook the kidneys till tender, 20 to 25 minutes. Add the flour paste and stir till the liquid has thickened. Taste for salt and pepper, sprinkle the parsley on top, and serve hot.

MAKES 4 TO 6 SERVINGS

chicken, onions, and bacon braised in zinfandel

This is an American version of French coq au vin by virtue of the tomato paste, the peppered bacon used in place of the more traditional *lardons,* and the spicy California Zinfandel wine. I think the dish equals the French classic on every count, and the bacon adds a distinctive flavor that never fails to impress.

3 tablespoons butter
18 very small white onions
1½ cups chicken broth
One 3½-pound chicken, cut into serving pieces
½ cup plus 2 tablespoons all-purpose flour
4 thick slices peppered bacon, cut into 1-inch pieces
1 cup Zinfandel or other spicy red wine
1 tablespoon tomato paste
2 garlic cloves, crushed
Herb bouquet (½ teaspoon dried thyme, 1 bay leaf, and 2 sprigs parsley wrapped in cheesecloth)
Salt and freshly ground black pepper to taste

• In a medium skillet, melt the butter over moderate heat, add the onions, and brown them lightly on all sides. Add ½ cup of the broth, reduce the heat to low, cover, and simmer the onions for 20 minutes. Set aside.

• On a plate, dredge the chicken pieces lightly in ½ cup of flour and set aside.

• In a large, deep skillet, fry the bacon over moderate heat and drain on paper towels. Add the chicken to the skillet, cook till golden brown on all sides, and transfer to a plate. Add the remaining 2 tablespoons of flour to the fat in the skillet and stir for 5 minutes. Add the wine, increase the heat, and stir to collect the brown bits on the bottom of the pan. Add the remaining 1 cup of broth plus the tomato paste and stir till well blended. Return the chicken to the skillet and add the onions and bacon, the garlic, the herb bouquet, and salt and pepper. Reduce the heat to low, cover, and simmer till the chicken is tender, about 45 minutes, adding more broth if necessary.

• Remove and discard the herb bouquet, transfer the chicken, onions, and bacon to a serving platter, and pour the sauce over the top. Serve hot.

MAKES 4 SERVINGS

southern-style smothered chicken with bacon and lemon slices

Throughout the American South, whole chickens are "smothered" in every way imaginable for both ultimate moistness and flavor, but this spicy version from the Carolina and Georgia Lowcountry is without question one of the most distinctive and delicious. Local cooks might well use very salty, heavily smoked "country-style" bacon made from the same hogs raised for country hams, but since this pungent bacon is an acquired taste for some and difficult to find outside the region, probably your best bet is an artisanal fruitwood-smoked bacon or ordinary hickory-smoked one found in most supermarkets. Feel free to experiment with all types of bacon for this dish.

½ pound streaky bacon slices, cut into 3-inch-long strips
10 fresh lemon slices, about ¼ inch thick
1 cup chicken broth
1 large onion, sliced
2 carrots, scraped and cut into ½-inch rounds
½ teaspoon dried thyme
½ teaspoon ground bay leaf
¼ teaspoon ground allspice
Pinch of grated fresh nutmeg
Salt and freshly ground black pepper to taste
One 3½-pound chicken, trussed with kitchen twine

• Arrange half the bacon strips in the bottom of a large, heavy pot or kettle, arrange the lemon slices over the top, then cover with the remaining bacon strips. Add half the broth, layer the onion slices and carrot rounds over the top, then sprinkle the thyme, bay leaf, allspice, nutmeg, and salt and pepper over the top.

• Position the whole chicken in the center of the pot, add the remaining broth, and bring to a boil. Reduce the heat to low, cover, and simmer till the chicken is tender, about 1 hour, basting it with the liquid every 15 minutes.

• To serve, remove the twine and either disjoint the chicken or carve it into serving portions, topping each portion with solids and liquid from the pot. Serve immediately.

MAKES 4 SERVINGS

italian roasted turkey breast stuffed with pancetta, raisins, and pine nuts

Unbeknownst to many Americans, turkey plays a major role in northern Italian cooking, and the many creative ways chefs there deal with the fowl are enough to make us hang our heads in shame. This particular preparation, which depends as much on spicy pancetta as on raisins and pine nuts for its distinctive savor, was served to me by a seasoned "mamma" while I was in Parma learning all about Parmigiano-Reggiano cheese. The dish does require a bit of time and effort, but I say the sumptuous results more than justify the means. For ultimate flavor, I do strongly recommend that you use dark turkey or chicken meat for the stuffing instead of the blander breast or wings.

½ cup seedless golden raisins
Dry vermouth
¼ pound ground turkey or chicken
¼ cup ground pork
¼ cup heavy cream
1 large egg
Salt and freshly ground black pepper to taste
3 ounces pancetta, chopped
¼ cup toasted pine nuts
One 2-pound boneless, skinless turkey breast
3 tablespoons olive oil
1 medium onion, chopped
1 carrot, scraped and chopped
½ teaspoon dried sage
1 cup dry white wine
3 tablespoons butter

• Place the raisins in a small bowl, add enough vermouth to cover, and let plump about 1 hour.

• In a blender or food processor, combine the ground turkey and pork, the cream, egg, and salt and pepper, purée the mixture, and scrape into a mixing bowl. Add the pancetta, pine nuts, and raisins and stir the stuffing till well blended.

• Spread out the turkey breast on a work surface, pound it with a mallet to about ¼ inch thick, and season with salt and pepper to taste. Spread the stuffing evenly over the breast, roll up the breast snugly, and tie securely with kitchen twine.

• Preheat the oven to 350°F.

• In a medium baking pan, heat the oil over moderate heat, add the turkey roll, and brown evenly on all sides. Transfer the roll to a plate, add the onion, carrot, and sage to the pan, and stir for 2 minutes. Add the wine and bring to a boil. Return the turkey roll to the pan, place in the oven, and roast, uncovered, till cooked through, about 1 hour, basting once or twice.

• Transfer the roll to a plate and cover to keep warm. Strain the liquid into a small saucepan, add the butter, and stir over low heat till the sauce is well blended.

• To serve, carve the turkey roll crosswise into ½-inch slices, arrange equal numbers of slices on serving plates, spoon a little sauce over the slices, and serve immediately.

MAKES 4 SERVINGS

BACON BONUS
Barding the breast of roasted fowl (or whole small game birds) with strips of bacon is a natural basting technique that keeps the bird moist. For a crisp, golden finish, remove the strips about 15 minutes before the end of cooking.

chicken and bacon succotash

I have no idea if the original American colonists added bacon to the lima bean and corn succotash introduced to them by the Indians, but it's for sure that no succotash enthusiast today would dream of making the concoction without a little fried bacon, either mixed into the other ingredients or sprinkled on top. Although succotash is traditionally served as a side dish to baked ham and outdoor barbecued items (especially in the South), I came up with the idea long ago of transforming the dish into a main course by adding shredded leftover chicken and the finest artisanal bacon I could find. Because of its unmistakable, assertive flavor, I'm normally very careful about using maple-smoked bacon, but for this succotash, it serves as the perfect complement—and that includes certain ordinary supermarket brands. Frozen (not canned) corn is fine for this dish, but fresh is nothing less than celestial.

2 cups fresh or frozen lima beans
5 thick slices maple-smoked bacon
2 medium onions, finely chopped
½ green bell pepper, seeded and finely chopped
1½ cups shredded cooked chicken
2½ cups milk
Salt and freshly ground black pepper to taste
Tabasco sauce to taste
2 cups fresh or frozen (and thawed) corn kernels
½ cup heavy cream

• Place the lima beans in a saucepan with enough water to cover. Bring to a boil, reduce the heat to moderate, cover, cook for 10 minutes, and drain.

• Meanwhile, fry the bacon over moderate heat in a large, deep skillet till crisp, drain on paper towels, and crumble. Drain off all but 2 tablespoons of fat from the skillet, add the onions and bell pepper, and stir till softened, about 5 minutes. Add the lima beans, chicken, milk, salt and pepper, and Tabasco, stir, and simmer till the milk is reduced, about 10 minutes. Add the corn and cream, stir, return to a simmer, and cook till the mixture has thickened but is not dry, watching carefully. Sprinkle on the bacon, stir, and serve hot.

MAKES 4 SERVINGS

french squabs with bacon and mushroom sauce

In France, a *poussin* is a full-flavored 1½- to 2-pound squab chicken most frequently baked *en cocotte* with onions, garlic, mushrooms, and always *lard fumé*, *lardons,* or another form of smoked bacon. The closest we have in the United States are the small, domesticated pigeons called squabs, available fresh or frozen in the best markets and often just as delicious as their French cousins. A regular 2-pound broiler chicken could certainly be substituted for the squabs in this recipe, but even if it's "free-range," it will not be as succulent. If you can find or order online genuine French smoked pork belly (*lard fumé* or *lard maigre*), so much the better.

½ pound slab bacon (rind removed), cut into small pieces
4 tablespoons (½ stick) butter
Two 1- to 1½-pound squabs (or very small chickens)
2 scallions (white parts only), minced
1 garlic clove, minced
½ pound mushrooms, quartered
1 cup dry white wine
1 cup beef broth
Salt and freshly ground black pepper to taste

• Preheat the oven to 350°F.
• In a 2-quart casserole, fry the bacon over moderate heat till crisp, transfer to a small bowl, and set aside. Add 2 tablespoons of the butter to the bacon grease and sear the squabs in the fat on all sides till golden brown, about 15 minutes. Transfer the squabs to a plate and set aside.
• Add the remaining 2 tablespoons of butter to the pot, add the scallions, garlic, and mushrooms, and stir till softened, about 3 minutes. Add the bacon, wine, broth, and salt and pepper and return the squabs to the pot, breast sides up. Cover the pot, place in the oven, and cook for 30 minutes. Uncover and continue to cook till the sauce has thickened slightly, about 20 minutes.
• Taste the sauce for salt and pepper and serve the squabs whole or disjointed, with the mushrooms and sauce spooned over each.

MAKES 2 SERVINGS

english roast guinea hens with bacon and mushrooms

Like partridge, pheasant, quail, and certain other game birds, guinea hen (or guinea fowl) tends to be dry and thus requires either barding (wrapping with some form of fat) or moist cooking, techniques that were perfected in English cookery centuries ago. As anyone knows who's ever ordered roast guinea hen at Rule's, Shepherd's, or other classic English restaurants in London, the dark, pleasantly gamy fowl is one of the most succulent on earth when combined with smoky bacon, currant jelly, and vegetables. Although you might find fresh birds at the most upscale butchers and markets, most in this country are frozen and perfectly acceptable. You can also prepare a large chicken in this manner, though the flavor cannot hold a candle to that of guinea hen. Also, if you can't find English or Irish bacon, use a good streaky one that has been lightly smoked.

2 tablespoons butter
2 tablespoons olive oil
Two 2-pound dressed guinea hens
4 slices English or Irish bacon, chopped
1 large onion, finely chopped
½ pound mushrooms, cut in half
1 cup dry red wine
2 tablespoons brandy
2½ cups chicken broth
3 tablespoons red currant jelly
Salt and freshly ground black pepper to taste

• Preheat the oven to 350°F.
• In a medium baking pan, heat the butter and olive oil over moderate heat, add the guinea hens, and brown on all sides. Cover the pan, roast the hens about 20 minutes, and transfer them to a plate.
• Add the bacon, onion, and mushrooms to the pan, stir over moderate heat till the vegetables are golden brown, about 8 minutes, and transfer to a plate. Add the wine, brandy, broth, and jelly to the pan, bring to a low boil, stirring, and cook till the sauce is reduced and thickened, about 20 minutes. Return the guinea hens, bacon, and vegetables to the pan and add salt and pepper. Bring to a boil, reduce the heat to low, cover, and simmer the hens till tender, about 25 minutes, basting them once or twice with the sauce.
• To serve, cut the hens in half with a heavy knife or kitchen scissors and serve hot with the sauce.

MAKES 4 SERVINGS

bacon-wrapped roasted quail stuffed with oysters

Numerous species of quail (bobwhite, mountain, Montezuma, redhead, Pharaoh) are either hunted or farm-raised throughout the United States, but no matter the type, if the small, succulent birds are not barded (wrapped with some form of fat) and/or stuffed before being roasted or grilled, they can be so dry as to be inedible. Here the problem is easily solved by stuffing the quail with moist fresh oysters and wrapping them with strips of streaky bacon, a classic technique that virtually guarantees both moisture and sublime flavor—so long, that is, as you baste them with the pan juices and don't overcook them. Once was the time when epicures would eat only fresh quail, but today the frozen birds found in many markets are just as prized.

8 dressed quail (fresh or frozen and thawed)
½ lemon
¾ cup (1½ sticks) melted butter
1½ tablespoons dried tarragon
Salt and freshly ground black pepper to taste
Tabasco sauce to taste
16 fresh oysters, shucked
2½ cups cornmeal
8 slices streaky applewood-smoked bacon
Boiled wild rice, buttered

• Preheat the oven to 450°F.
• Rinse the quail well inside and out and pat dry with paper towels.
• Squeeze the lemon into the butter, add the tarragon, salt and pepper, and Tabasco, and stir. Dip the oysters into the butter mixture, dredge lightly in the cornmeal on a plate, and stuff two into the cavity of each quail. Wrap each quail with a slice of bacon and secure the bacon, wings, and legs close to the body with a metal skewer.
• Place the quail on a rack in a large shallow roasting pan and roast for 15 minutes. Baste the birds with the pan juices and continue roasting for 10 minutes longer, basting once more. Serve 2 quail per person with wild rice.

MAKES 4 SERVINGS

baked marinated quail

Marinated quail that are lightly browned, barded with streaky bacon, and baked with the marinade are not only eminently delicious but just as moist and tender as any properly cooked birds should be. Because of the flavor complexities in the marinade, this is one time when I use only simply cured supermarket bacon that has enough lean meat for texture and fat for self-basting. These quail, of course, can be prepared for just a casual dinner, but since they are rather elegant, I also like to arrange them on toast triangles surrounded by wild rice and steamed asparagus and present everything on a large silver platter.

12 dressed quail (fresh or frozen and thawed)
Salt and freshly ground black pepper to taste
½ cup gin
½ cup peanut oil
2 scallions (part of green leaves included), chopped
1 cup chopped celery leaves
2 teaspoon dried tarragon, crumbled
Tabasco sauce to taste
8 tablespoons (1 stick) butter
12 slices streaky bacon
12 toast triangles

• Season each quail inside and out with salt and pepper and arrange them in a single layer in a large baking dish. In a medium bowl, whisk together the gin and oil till well blended, add the scallions, celery leaves, tarragon, and Tabasco, and stir well. Pour the marinade over the quail, cover with plastic wrap, and refrigerate about 4 hours, turning the quail once or twice.

• Preheat the oven to 350°F.

• Remove the quail from the marinade and wipe dry with paper towels. Melt half the butter in a large cast-iron skillet over moderate heat, add half the quail, lightly brown them on all sides, and transfer back to the baking dish. Repeat with the remaining butter and quail. Wrap each quail snugly with a slice of bacon, strain the marinade over the birds, cover with a sheet of aluminum foil, and bake till the quail are very tender, 30 to 35 minutes.

• On a large silver serving platter, arrange each quail on a toast triangle and serve hot.

MAKES 6 SERVINGS

belgium braised rabbit, prunes, and bacon in beer

Rabbit (wild or domesticated) braised in fruity, hoppy beer is popular all over Belgium, but when it's combined with prunes, smoky bacon, and the unique red Rodenbach beer of Flanders, the gustatory experience is astounding. Available in many of our markets, Trappist beer can be used as an acceptable substitute, as well as any full-bodied English ale. While it's still not easy in this country to find fresh rabbits, the frozen, which are dressed and usually cut into pieces, are a very good product so long as each weighs at least 2½ pounds and is meaty. Do test the rabbit after about 1½ hours of simmering to make sure it's still well-textured and not overcooked and dry.

1 pound pitted prunes
¼ pound slab bacon (rind removed), cut into pieces
5 tablespoons all-purpose flour
Salt and freshly ground black pepper to taste
Two frozen and thawed 2½-pound rabbits, disjointed
4 medium onions, chopped
2 carrots, scraped and chopped
2 garlic cloves, minced
Two 12-ounce bottles dark beer or ale
2 tablespoons cider vinegar
¼ teaspoon dried thyme, crumbled
2 bay leaves
2 whole cloves

- Place the prunes in a bowl with just enough warm water to cover and let soak for 1 hour.
- In a large, heavy pot, fry the bacon over moderate heat till most of the fat is rendered and drain on paper towels. On a plate, mix together 3 tablespoons of the flour and the salt and pepper and dredge the rabbit pieces in the mixture, tapping off excess flour. In batches, brown the rabbit on all sides in the bacon fat and transfer the pieces to a plate.
- Add the onions, carrots, and garlic to the pot and stir till softened, about 5 minutes. Return the rabbit to the pot, sprinkle the remaining 2 tablespoons of flour over the top, and cook about 5 minutes longer, turning the pieces. Gradually add the beer, allowing the sauce to thicken slightly before adding more. Add the vinegar, thyme, bay leaves, and cloves, reduce the heat to low, cover, and simmer for 45 minutes. Add the prunes and bacon, cover, and simmer till the rabbit is very tender, about 30 minutes. Remove the bay leaves and serve the rabbit hot.

MAKES 6 SERVINGS

new england clam hash

Prepared all along the New England coast with both hard-shell quahog clams and soft-shell steamers, this classic hash illustrates how, when it comes to flavoring certain dishes, bacon grease is as important as the bacon itself. I love the bold taste and aroma of maple-smoked bacon in this hash, but equally good (and regional) is cob-smoked. Serve the hash for brunch or a casual supper with lots of fat radishes and other raw vegetables and some form of cornbread.

6 thick maple- or cob-smoked bacon
2 tablespoons butter plus 1 tablespoon softened butter
1 medium onion, finely chopped
2 medium potatoes, diced and boiled till tender
3 cups minced fresh clams
2 tablespoons fresh chopped chives
Salt and freshly ground black pepper to taste
Tabasco sauce to taste
4 large egg yolks
1 cup heavy cream

• In a large, heavy skillet, fry the bacon over moderate heat till crisp, drain on paper towels, and crumble.

• Pour off all but 2 tablespoons of grease from the skillet and add the 2 tablespoons of butter. Add the onion, stir for 2 minutes, add the potatoes, and cook till the underside of the mixture is golden, about 3 minutes. Add the clams, chives, salt and pepper, and Tabasco, cook for 2 minutes, then press the mixture down firmly with a spatula.

• Preheat the oven broiler.

• In a bowl, beat together the egg yolks and cream, pour over the clam mixture, cover the skillet and cook till the eggs are just set, about 2 minutes. Dot the surface with the softened butter, brown the top under the broiler, loosen the edges with the spatula, and slide the hash onto a heated platter. Sprinkle the crumbled bacon over the top and serve immediately.

MAKES 4 SERVINGS

louisiana shrimp creole

In Louisiana Creole cookery, bacon is an essential ingredient not only in smothered chicken, eggplant au gratin, oyster pie, and braised quail but also in this classic shrimp dish, which is always served with boiled rice. On home territory, shrimp Creole is often made with the heavily smoked "country-style" or salty "Cajun bacon" (pickled pork shoulder cured in brine) found in most local markets. Given the difficulty of obtaining these products outside the region, however, I recommend fairly thick slices of double-smoked bacon. Also, if you have access to three or four home-grown tomatoes (peeled, juices included), by all means use these instead of the canned ones. Just make sure not to overcook the shrimp—they're ready when they turn pink and curl.

2 thick slices double-smoked bacon, cut into tiny bits
2 medium onions, chopped
2 celery ribs, chopped
1 medium green bell pepper, seeded and chopped
1 garlic clove, minced
One 28-ounce can whole tomatoes with their juices, chopped
¼ teaspoon dried basil, crumbled
1 bay leaf
Salt and freshly ground black pepper to taste
2 teaspoons Worcestershire sauce
Tabasco sauce to taste
1 pound fresh medium shrimp, shelled and deveined
Boiled rice

• In a large, heavy pot, fry the bacon over moderate heat till crisp and drain on paper towels. Add the onions, celery, bell pepper, and garlic to the pot and stir about 4 minutes. Add the tomatoes and their juices, the basil, bay leaf, salt and pepper, Worcestershire, and Tabasco and stir well. Bring to a low simmer, cover, and cook till the mixture thickens, 25 to 30 minutes. Add the shrimp and bacon and stir. Return to a simmer and cook, uncovered, just till the shrimp turn pink and curl, about 8 minutes.

• To serve, place mounds of rice on serving plates, make wide wells in the mounds, and spoon the shrimp into the wells. Serve piping hot.

MAKES 4 SERVINGS

baked oysters with mustard greens and bacon

With so much distinctive artisanal bacon now being produced in the United States, it's little wonder that more and more gifted professional chefs are using it to create unusual dishes. Frank Stitt, owner/chef at Highlands Bar and Grill in Birmingham, Alabama, is such an innovator, and perhaps none of his dishes better illustrates the transforming power of a superior bacon than these baked oysters with a peppery topping of mustard greens and bacon. If you're unable to find young, crisp, deep-green mustard greens, an acceptable substitute is a combination of fresh spinach and watercress.

¼ pound hickory- or applewood-smoked bacon, finely diced
1 medium onion, finely diced
2 garlic cloves, finely diced
1 small hot red chile pepper, seeded and finely chopped
4 cups loosely packed, washed, drained, and finely chopped mustard greens
Zest and juice of 1 lemon
8 tablespoons (1 stick) butter, cut into pieces
Salt and freshly ground black pepper to taste
2 dozen fresh oysters on the half shell
1 cup coarse white bread crumbs

• In a large skillet, fry the bacon over moderate heat till almost crisp and drain on paper towels.

• Add the onion to the skillet, reduce the heat to low, and stir till very soft but not browned, about 7 minutes. Add the garlic and chile pepper and stir 2 minutes longer. Add the mustard greens, lemon zest and juice, bacon, butter, and salt and pepper and toss and stir till the butter has melted and the greens are well coated.

• Preheat the oven to 500°F.

• Place a small amount of greens on each oyster and sprinkle bread crumbs on top of each. Arrange the oysters on a heavy baking sheet and bake till the crumbs are golden and the oysters heated through, about 5 minutes. Serve immediately.

MAKES 4 SERVINGS

norwegian bacon-wrapped broiled salmon

Norwegian chefs might use lean Danish back bacon for this popular dish, but although this bacon is very flavorful, I find it simply doesn't have enough fat to baste the fish adequately while cooking. If you do want to try Danish (or English) bacon, search for some that has fatty ends; otherwise, I recommend regular streaky bacon. Traditionally in Norway, this salmon is served with boiled parsleyed potatoes or dilled lentils, thin rye bread or crisps, and either shot glasses of ice-cold aquavit or beer—or both.

¼ cup grainy mustard
2 tablespoons minced fresh dill
Salt to taste
2 tablespoons crushed peppercorns
Four 6-ounce skinless fresh salmon fillets
4 slices streaky bacon

- Preheat the oven broiler.
- In a small bowl, combine the mustard, dill, salt, and peppercorns and mix till well blended. Spread equal amounts of the mixture over the curved sides of the salmon fillets, pressing down the peppercorns slightly with the knife blade. Lay a bacon slice lengthwise over the top of each fillet and tuck the ends underneath as snugly as possible. Thread a metal skewer through the length of each fillet to secure the edges of the bacon.
- On the rack of a broiler pan, arrange the fillets bacon sides down, pressing down the loose top edges of the bacon, and broil 4 inches from the heat about 4 minutes. Turn the fillets over and broil till the fish is just cooked through and the bacon is crisp, 3 to 4 minutes longer. Serve immediately.

MAKES 4 SERVINGS

canadian salmon, potato, and bacon torte

Similar in concept to the *tourtières* of Quebec, the many savory tortes, pies, and loaves of western Canada's British Columbia and Alberta provinces use not only the wealth of Chinook, coho, sockeye, and other Pacific salmon that spawn in the Fraser River but also the region's lean, superior peameal (or "back") bacon, which is usually coated with cornmeal. Rarely is this authentic Canadian bacon marketed in the United States (although it can be ordered from a few sources on the Internet), forcing serious bacon lovers to stock up when visiting our northern neighbor. Salmon and bacon is still another of those sacred marriages that demand the best-quality ingredients, so do look for the freshest fish and most reputable Canadian bacon (as well as the youngest potatoes) for this dish.

4½ cups all-purpose flour
4 teaspoons baking powder
2 teaspoons salt
2 cups lard, diced
¾ cup boiling water
4 teaspoons lemon juice
1 large egg, beaten
2 tablespoons butter
6 medium slices Canadian bacon, cut into 1-inch pieces
1 medium onion, chopped
2 cups peeled potatoes cut into ½-inch cubes
One 1-pound salmon steak, boned, skinned, and cut into ½-inch pieces
Salt and freshly ground black pepper to taste

• In a large mixing bowl, combine the flour, baking powder, salt, and half of the diced lard and mix till well blended. Place the remaining 1 cup of lard in a small bowl, add the boiling water, stir well till lard is melted, and let cool slightly. Add the lemon juice and egg, blend well, pour the mixture over the flour mixture, and stir thoroughly to form a smooth dough. Turn out the dough on a lightly floured surface, knead lightly, wrap in plastic wrap, and chill for 1 hour.

• Preheat the oven to 400°F. Butter a 9-by-2-inch baking dish and set aside.

• In a large, heavy skillet, melt the butter over moderate heat, add the bacon, and stir till slightly browned. Add the onion and stir 2 minutes. Add the potatoes and stir for 1 minute. Add just enough water to cover, bring to a low boil, and cook till the potatoes are tender and some of the water has evaporated, about 15 minutes. Remove from the heat, add the salmon and salt and pepper, stir, and let the mixture cool.

• On a work surface, roll out half the chilled dough about ¼ inch thick, line the prepared baking dish with the dough, and fill the shell with the salmon mixture. Roll out the remaining dough, lay it over the filling, seal the edges by pressing them down with a fork, and cut several slits on top. Bake the torte for 15 minutes, reduce the heat to 350°F, and continue baking till the crust is golden, about 30 minutes longer.

• Cut and serve the hot torte in wedges.

MAKES 6 SERVINGS

BACON BANTER
"If you eat much bacon, save the fat, and pour it always into a metal container and then pour water over it. The burned food particles will sink into the water, and the fat will rise as it cools and be clean and easy to lift into another cup or bowl."
—M.F.K. FISHER, *HOW TO COOK A WOLF*, 1942

basque salt cod with bacon and tomatoes

While *bacalao a la vizcaína* is a specialty of Spain's Basque region, the classic dish is found today virtually all over the country. Originally salted and dried for long storage, mild, lean, firm salt cod is the ideal fish for slow simmering and most often seen in our better markets stacked upright in baskets at the seafood counter. In Spain, bacalao would most likely be prepared with lean, nutty, smoked *tocino* bacon, but since that exquisite product is not yet available in this country, I recommend an artisanal hickory-smoked bacon. Likewise, since the sweet Basque peppers called *noras* are strictly regional, I find pimentos to be the best substitute.

1 pound filleted salt cod
1 cup chopped drained pimentos
One 28-ounce can plum tomatoes, coarsely chopped and juice included
¼ teaspoon cayenne pepper
⅓ cup all-purpose flour
4 thick, lean slices hickory-smoked bacon, cut into 1-inch pieces
2 tablespoons olive oil
1 large onion, chopped
1 garlic clove, minced

• Place the cod in a large glass dish or bowl with enough cold water to cover and let soak 24 hours, changing the water several times.

• In a blender or food processor, purée the pimentos, ¼ cup of juice from the tomatoes, and the cayenne and set aside.

• Drain the cod and cut or break it into 1½-inch pieces, removing any bones or skin. Place the pieces in a bowl with the flour and toss till the pieces are well coated.

• In a large, heavy skillet, fry the bacon over moderate heat till crisp and transfer to a large bowl. Add 1 tablespoon of the oil to the skillet, brown the cod pieces on all sides in the fat, and add them to the bacon. Add the remaining 1 tablespoon of oil to the skillet, add the onion and garlic, and stir about 3 minutes. Add the reserved pimento mixture, the tomatoes and their remaining juices, the cod and bacon mixture, and stir well. Reduce the heat to low, cover the skillet, and simmer the mixture for 1 hour. Serve hot.

MAKES 4 TO 6 SERVINGS

vegetables
and fruits

Corn with Bell Peppers and Bacon

Bacon-and-Mushroom-Stuffed Vidalia Onions

Brussels Sprouts Braised with Apple and Bacon

Pearl's Cauliflower with Bacon, Pimentos, and Sunflower Seeds

Burgundian Carrots with Onions, Bacon, and Black Currants

Georgia Okra, Tomato, and Bacon Mull

Black Forest Mushrooms with Bacon and Cheese

Colombian Potatoes with Bacon-Cheese Sauce

South American Yams with Prunes and Bacon

French Gratin of Potatoes, Bacon, and Cheese

French Cabbage and Bacon Troisgros

Irish Colcannon

Russian Creamed Sauerkraut with Bacon and Shiitakes

Italian Radicchio Smothered with Pancetta

Chinese Stir-Fried Greens and Bacon

Smoky Hoppin' John

Authentic Boston Baked Beans with Bacon

English Faggots and Split Peas

Swiss Apple, Pear, Potato, and Bacon Braise

Swedish Apple Wedges and Onions with Bacon

corn with bell peppers and bacon

You might consider this simple but wonderful mélange to be a variation on succotash without the lima beans were it not for the distinctive flavoring of vinegar and jolt of cayenne pepper. What the dish proves over and over is that the combination of corn, bell pepper, and smoky bacon is still another of those culinary marriages that is forever sacred, and if ever there were an opportunity to experiment with all types of artisanal and foreign bacons, this is it. You could, I suppose, use frozen corn, but rest assured the results will not be the same.

4 large ears fresh corn
4 slices cob-smoked bacon, diced
1 medium onion, chopped
1 small green bell pepper, cored, seeded, and diced
1 small red bell pepper, cored, seeded, and diced
1 tablespoon red wine vinegar
Salt and freshly ground black pepper to taste
Cayenne pepper to taste

• Place the corn in a large pot with enough water to cover, bring to a boil, and drain. With a sharp knife, cut the kernels from the ears (there should be about 2 cups) and set aside.

• In a medium skillet, fry the bacon over moderate heat till almost crisp and drain all but 2 tablespoons of fat from the skillet. Add the onion and bell peppers and stir till fully softened, 8 to 10 minutes. Add the corn, vinegar, salt and pepper, and cayenne and stir the mixture till it is well combined. Serve hot.

MAKES 4 SERVINGS

BACON BUZZ
In the early twentieth century, American Midwestern hog farmers began crossbreeding fatty Poland China pigs ("lard pigs") with leaner English Berkshire ones ("bacon pigs") to produce the standard of bacon we know today.

bacon-and-mushroom-stuffed vidalia onions

Now available in most markets throughout early summer, sweet Georgia Vidalia onions are, along with Mauis from Hawaii and Walla Wallas from Washington State, the aristocrats of the large onion family. And when you stuff and bake them with a smoky artisanal bacon, mushrooms, and a noble cheese, you have a dish that not only complements any roasted meats or fowl but can also be proudly served on its own at brunch with either cold cuts or, in fine Southern tradition, ham biscuits. One nice thing about this recipe is you can prepare the onions in advance, stuff and bake them for the initial twenty minutes, then finish them off shortly before serving. This is also another perfect opportunity to experiment with different smoked bacons.

4 medium Vidalia onions
4 thick slices applewood-smoked bacon, finely chopped
½ pound mushrooms, finely chopped
½ cup soft bread crumbs
4 ounces Emmentaler cheese, grated
2 tablespoons chopped fresh parsley leaves
Salt and freshly ground black pepper to taste
½ cup chicken broth

• Peel the onions, cut off the root ends, and, with a sharp paring knife, hollow out each one to within ¼ inch of the sides, trimming the edges to make a wide, even opening. Arrange the onion shells in a medium baking dish, finely chop the onion pulp, and set aside.

• In a large skillet, fry the bacon over moderate heat till almost crisp, add the chopped onions and mushrooms, and stir till the vegetables are golden, about 10 minutes. Add the bread crumbs, 2 tablespoons of the cheese, the parsley, and salt and pepper and stir till the cheese begins to melt, about 5 minutes.

• Preheat the oven to 400°F.

• Stuff the onion shells with equal amounts of the mixture, pour the broth into the bottom of the dish, cover with foil, and bake 20 minutes. Uncover, sprinkle the tops with the remaining cheese, and bake till golden brown, about 20 minutes longer. Serve hot.

MAKES 4 SERVINGS

brussels sprouts braised with apple and bacon

I admit that I was never fond of Brussels sprouts (like so many people) till one fall day when a neighbor handed me a fresh stalk lined with tiny, compact sprouts she'd picked up at a farmers market and told me how she cooked them with apple and bacon. The transformation was amazing, with the sweet apple taming the slight bitterness of the sprouts and the smoky bacon (meat and fat) adding a flavor dimension that was almost elegant. I still reject frozen sprouts as too strong for my taste, and have learned that even the small, bright green, fresh ones can't be held in the refrigerator for more than about three days without developing an offensive piquancy. But truly fresh Brussels sprouts, available throughout the cold months in better markets and cooked in this manner, are now a real treat for me—and my guests.

1 quart fresh Brussels sprouts
2 slices lean hickory-smoked bacon, cut into small pieces
1 tablespoon butter
1 cooking apple, cored and cut into chunks
2 teaspoons lemon juice
Salt and freshly ground black pepper to taste
Pinch of grated nutmeg

• Remove and discard any wilted leaves from the Brussels sprouts, trim off the stems (but not too close or the sprouts will fall apart), cut an X in the base of each sprout, and set aside.

• In a large, heavy skillet (not cast-iron), fry the bacon over moderate heat till it releases its fat, add the butter to the fat, add the Brussels sprouts, and stir gently till they begin to brown, about 10 minutes. Add the apple and lemon juice, season with salt and pepper and nutmeg, cover, reduce the heat to low, and cook till the sprouts are tender and the apple has softened, 10 to 15 minutes. Serve hot.

MAKES 4 TO 6 SERVINGS

pearl's cauliflower with bacon, pimentos, and sunflower seeds

One of my early mentors, Pearl Byrd Foster, created some of America's most innovative dishes at her tiny family-style restaurant in New York called Mr. & Mrs. Foster's Place, and one of her most amazing was this silky cauliflower enhanced by crunchy sunflower seeds, strips of pimento, and streaky, house-cured bacon that she personally selected a couple of times a week at a specialty butcher shop on Second Avenue. Pearl liked to present the whole cauliflower surrounded by steamed green beans on a platter, then serve the florets with the garnish. Never before tasting this dish did I realize how crumbled bacon can transform this rather bland vegetable into such a flavorful masterpiece, and since then, I've experimented with many different smoked and unsmoked styles. Sometimes I've even added a little of the bacon fat to the melted butter.

8 lean slices streaky bacon
1 medium head cauliflower (about 2 pounds), trimmed and washed
2 tablespoons lemon juice
2½ cups milk, scalded
1 teaspoon salt
Freshly ground black pepper to taste
½ cup toasted sunflower seeds
One 4-ounce jar pimento strips, drained
6 tablespoons (¾ stick) butter, melted

• In a skillet, fry the bacon over moderate heat till crisp, drain on paper towels, and crumble.

• Place the cauliflower bottom side down in a heavy pot, sprinkle with the lemon juice, and pour the milk over the top. Bring the milk to a very low boil, cover the pot, and simmer till the cauliflower is tender, about 25 minutes.

• Remove the cauliflower from the pot, drain well, and place in a serving bowl. Season with salt and pepper, then scatter the sunflower seeds over the top. Arrange the pimento strips attractively over the top, spoon the melted butter over the entire head, and sprinkle the crumbled bacon over the top. Serve the cauliflower florets hot.

MAKES 4 TO 6 SERVINGS

burgundian carrots with onions, bacon, and black currants

As in the United States, there's lots of hoopla these days in many areas of France about the tender (and often tasteless) baby carrots found in so many markets (at inflated prices), but travel through Burgundy and what you still see mostly (in both home kitchens and restaurants) are the bright, mature, full-flavored carrots that have always been one of the region's special gifts of nature. And leave it to the Burgundians to enhance this root vegetable by cooking it with either smoked or unsmoked *lardons* and the area's legendary black currants (the same currants used to make the cordial known as *crème de cassis* and delectable preserves). Unfortunately, fresh currants are not available in many parts of the United States due to their susceptibility to white pine disease, so if you're unable to find them during the summer months, substitute dark seedless raisins.

1 pound medium carrots, scraped and cut into ½-inch rounds
3 ounces lean slab bacon (rind removed), finely diced
12 tiny white onions, peeled
2 tablespoons fresh black currants
1 tablespoon all-purpose flour
½ cup chicken broth
Salt and freshly ground black pepper to taste
2 tablespoons butter

• Place the carrots in a saucepan with enough water to cover, bring to a boil, reduce the heat to low, cover, and simmer till the carrots are just tender, about 8 minutes. Drain and set aside.

• In a large saucepan, fry the bacon over moderate heat just till it renders its fat, add the onions, and stir gently till they are golden, about 10 minutes. Add the carrots and currants and stir till well blended. Sprinkle the flour over the top and stir about 1 minute. Add the broth, return to a simmer, and cook, uncovered, till the liquid has evaporated, about 10 minutes. Add the salt and pepper and butter and stir gently till the carrots are nicely glazed. Serve hot.

MAKES 6 SERVINGS

georgia okra, tomato, and bacon mull

While the affinity of okra and tomatoes is well known throughout the American South, the tradition in Georgia is to mull (slowly simmer) the vegetables with onions, plenty of smoky bacon, and one or two fresh herbs. I've learned that even those who are squeamish about the viscous texture of okra find this way of preparing the pods not just palatable but utterly delicious—the perfect side dish for pork chops and virtually any meat or fowl barbecued on the grill. Just be sure to select fresh okra that are small, dark green, slightly fuzzy, and not at all spotted, and when trimming off the stems, remember never to cut into the pods.

2 pounds fresh small okra, washed and stems removed
6 slices lean bacon (any style), cut into small pieces
2 medium onions, chopped
6 large, ripe tomatoes, peeled and chopped
1 tablespoon fresh thyme leaves
2 teaspoons salt
Freshly ground black pepper to taste
Tabasco sauce to taste

• Place the okra in a large saucepan, add enough water to cover, bring to a boil, reduce the heat to moderately low, and simmer till tender, about 10 minutes. Drain the okra in a colander.

• In a large skillet, fry the bacon over moderate heat till crisp and drain on paper towels. Pour off all but 2 tablespoons of the grease, add the onions, and stir for about 10 minutes. Add the tomatoes, thyme, and salt, season with pepper and Tabasco, stir well, reduce the heat to low, and simmer till the tomatoes are soft, about 20 minutes. Add the okra and bacon, stir gently, and simmer about 10 minutes longer before serving hot.

MAKES 6 SERVINGS

BACON BONUS
To reduce splattering while frying bacon, fit a wire-mesh splatter screen—available in kitchen supply shops and in many supermarkets—over the skillet.

black forest mushrooms with bacon and cheese

The Black Forest of Germany is known not only for its superior bacon (and hams) but as a major natural habitat of wild cèpe mushrooms (*Steinpilze*). I've eaten my share of them both in numerous guises during my occasional trips to Baden-Baden to undergo one *Kur* or another in the thermal baths, but what I really raved about one evening in the old-world dining room of the stately Brenner's Park Hotel were these sublime mushrooms with smoky Black Forest bacon that accompanied a succulent roasted guinea hen. Since then, I've also made the dish with fresh morels, chanterelles, shiitakes, and even chunks of huge portabellas, but what I never replace is the mellow German *Speck* or double-smoked slab bacon needed to reinforce the earthy savor of the mushrooms. Serve this dish with any roasted fowl or even a juicy steak.

3 thick slices Black Forest *Speck* or double-smoked slab bacon (rind removed), coarsely chopped
3 tablespoons butter
2 medium onions, chopped
2 pounds fresh cèpe mushrooms, cut into quarters
½ cup heavy cream
¼ pound Emmentaler cheese, grated
Freshly ground black pepper to taste
2 tablespoons chopped fresh parsley leaves

• In a large heavy skillet, fry the bacon over moderate heat till almost crisp, add the butter and onions, and stir till the onions soften, about 5 minutes. Add the mushrooms, stir well, and cook till the mushrooms begin to render their liquid, about 8 minutes. Cover the skillet, reduce the heat to low, and simmer the mixture for 30 minutes.

• Stirring constantly, gradually add the cream, then the cheese and pepper. Increase the heat slightly and stir till the cheese melts and the sauce is smooth. Transfer to a serving platter, sprinkle the parsley on top, and serve hot.

MAKES 4 TO 6 SERVINGS

colombian potatoes with bacon-cheese sauce

Since potatoes are indigenous to South America and were cultivated by the ancient Incas thousands of years ago, it's little wonder that the soups, stews, salads, breads, and cakes made with *papas* in Colombia, Ecuador, and Peru are countless. This particular preparation is a specialty of Bogotá and depends as much on lusty bacon as on a full-flavored Manchego, Roncal, or Castellano cheese for its distinction. If you can find savory golden-fleshed potatoes in a Latin American market, so much the better, and if Spanish cheeses are unavailable, use a slightly aged Münster or even a sharp cheddar. I like to serve these potatoes with a variety of grilled sausages and a sturdy red wine such as Chilean Cabernet.

6 large Idaho potatoes
4 slices streaky bacon, cut into small bits
1 medium onion, finely chopped
3 ripe medium tomatoes, peeled, seeded, and chopped
Salt and freshly ground black pepper to taste
¼ cup heavy cream
1 cup grated Manchego cheese

• Place the potatoes in a large pot and add enough water to cover. Bring to a boil, reduce the heat to a low boil, and cook till just tender, about 25 minutes. Drain the potatoes, peel, and keep warm.

• In a medium skillet, fry the bacon over moderate heat till almost crisp, add the onion, and stir about 2 minutes. Add the tomatoes and salt and pepper, reduce the heat to low, and simmer till the mixture is well blended and smooth, about 10 minutes, stirring occasionally. Add the cream and cheese and stir till the cheese melts and the sauce is very smooth.

• To serve, cut the potatoes into quarters, place 4 quarters on each plate, and spoon sauce over the top of each portion.

MAKES 6 SERVINGS

south american yams with prunes and bacon

Despite the persistent erroneous references to yams through United States markets, cookbooks, and food magazines, these multisized, multicolored tubers are native only to South and Central America and parts of Asia and Africa and are *not* the same as our sweet potatoes—which have considerably less sugar and moisture content. Genuine yams can be found in our Latin American markets (in colors that range from ivory to pink to purple), and from Venezuela down to Chile, they are routinely combined with dried fruits and some form of bacon in any number of classic dishes. Sweet potatoes can certainly be substituted for yams in this recipe, but for optimal flavor, I do suggest you use a mellow double-smoked bacon instead of the regular streaky product—preferably with equal proportions of fat and lean meat.

4 medium yams or sweet potatoes (about 2 pounds)
6 slices double-smoked bacon, cut into small pieces
2 tablespoons butter
⅓ cup water
3 tablespoons dry sherry
6 pitted prunes, finely chopped
Salt and freshly ground black pepper to taste

• Peel the yams, cut them into ¾-inch cubes, and place in a medium saucepan with enough water to cover. Bring to a boil, cook about 8 minutes, drain, and pat them dry.

• In a large, heavy skillet, fry the bacon over moderate heat till crisp, drain on paper towels, and crumble. Pour off all but about 3 tablespoons of fat from the skillet, add the butter, and heat till the fat foams. Add the yams and stir till they are barely tender, 3 to 5 minutes. Add the water, sherry, and prunes, bring to a low boil, and simmer till the liquid has evaporated, about 8 minutes. Add the crumbled bacon and salt and pepper, stir till well blended, and serve hot.

MAKES 4 SERVINGS

french gratin of potatoes, bacon, and cheese

In France's alpine Dauphiné region, a potato gratin involves nothing more than potatoes, cream, and maybe a little garlic; over in Savoie, Gruyère or Emmentaler cheese is usually added; while up in the rugged Franche-Comté, cooks go a step further by including *lardons* of smoked pork belly along with everything else. The secret of any potato gratin is slow baking at a relatively low temperature so the potatoes gradually absorb the cream and take on a silky texture. This requires not only adding the cream in separate measures but also basting the potatoes regularly to prevent browning till the very end. It may take a bit of careful watching and practice, but the goal is to produce potatoes that remain creamy soft with a crispy crust on top. The ideal cheese for this gratin is a nutty Comté, but if that's not available, use either Swiss Emmentaler or Gruyère.

1 garlic clove, peeled and cut in half
4 ounces slab bacon, cut into small pieces
6 russet potatoes (about 3 pounds)
Salt and freshly ground black pepper to taste
3 tablespoons butter
3 ounces Comté cheese, grated
4 cups half-and-half

• Preheat the oven to 300°F. Rub the garlic over the bottom and sides of a 2½- to 3-quart oval earthenware or ceramic gratin dish and let dry.

• In a medium skillet, fry the bacon over moderate heat till almost crisp, transfer to a plate, and reserve both the bacon and grease.

• Peel the potatoes and cut them into ⅛-inch rounds with a mandoline or sharp knife. Grease the dish with a little of the bacon grease, arrange a third of the potato rounds, overlapping, on the bottom, and season with salt and pepper. Dot with 1 tablespoon of the butter cut into pieces and sprinkle a third of the bacon and cheese each over the top. Repeat, layering with the remaining potatoes, butter, bacon, and cheese, and seasoning with salt and pepper. Pour 2 cups of the half-and-half over the top and bake in the middle of the oven for 45 minutes, breaking the bubbles and basting the potatoes with a large spoon from time to time.

• Add another cup of the half-and-half and continue baking for 20 minutes, breaking bubbles and basting. Add the remaining cup of half-and-half and continue baking till the potatoes are still moist and the top is golden brown, about 20 minutes. Serve piping hot.

MAKES 6 SERVINGS

french cabbage and bacon troisgros

Over the years, some of my greatest meals in France have been at Troisgros, in the small, nondescript southern-central town of Roanne, but the one that still sings most in my memory included a succulent roasted pigeon in liver sauce accompanied by this phenomenal braised cabbage flavored with crispy *lardons* and a buttery vinegar sauce. I think the late Jean Troisgros told me his *lardons* were made with pure salt pork, but when I prepare the cabbage today, I prefer to use meat that has a bit of lean (or "streak-o'-lean")—that or rather fatty slab bacon. Also, whereas Jean braised the cabbage in only water, I like the added flavor of chicken broth. Either way, you'll never view cabbage the same way once you've made it with this sublime sauce.

1 large head green cabbage (about 2½ pounds)
Salt
1 tablespoon olive oil
6 ounces lean salt pork (rind removed)
¼ cup chicken broth
¼ cup red wine vinegar
4 tablespoons (½ stick) butter, cut into pieces
Freshly ground black pepper to taste

• Remove the leaves from the head of cabbage, discard any discolored ones, and rinse the leaves. Bring a large kettle of salted water to a boil, add the leaves, blanch them about 8 minutes, and drain. Rinse the leaves in cold water, drain again, then chop them coarsely.

• Preheat the oven to 400°F.

• In a skillet, heat the olive oil over moderate heat, add the salt pork, stir till browned on all sides, about 8 minutes, and drain on paper towels.

• Place the cabbage in a heavy 2-quart casserole or pot, sprinkle the broth over the top, cover, and bake till all the broth has evaporated, 25 to 30 minutes, watching carefully to make sure the cabbage doesn't dry out and burn.

• In a small saucepan, boil the vinegar till reduced by half, gradually add the butter, and stir till well blended. Pour the mixture over the cabbage, add the salt pork, toss well, cover the casserole, and simmer over low heat 5 to 10 minutes. Season with pepper and serve hot.

MAKES 4 SERVINGS

irish colcannon

Known in England as "bubble and squeak," colcannon is a peasant Irish dish that can be traced back to the Middle Ages and is traditionally served with roasted meats on Halloween. It is made with either cabbage or kale or a combination of the two greens, and home cooks are just as likely to use such regional fatty cuts of bacon as "collars," "skipper joints," and "forehocks" as the meatier and better-known Irish (or "back") bacon. Personally, I could easily make a meal of colcannon, so long, that is, as it's crusty brown. In more practical terms, nothing goes better with a standing beef rib roast.

4 medium potatoes (about 2 pounds), peeled and cut into quarters
4 tablespoons (½ stick) butter
6 ounces Irish or English bacon, cut into small pieces
1 medium head green cabbage (about 2 pounds), discolored leaves discarded, cored, and shredded
½ cup chicken broth
Salt and freshly ground black pepper to taste

• Place the potatoes in a medium saucepan with enough water to cover. Bring to a boil, reduce the heat to low, cover, and cook till the potatoes are very tender, 20 to 25 minutes. Drain, mash in a large mixing bowl, and set aside.

• In a large skillet, melt 1 tablespoon of the butter over moderate heat, add the bacon, and fry till slightly browned, about 7 minutes. With a slotted spoon, transfer the bacon to a plate, add the cabbage to the skillet, and toss well. Cover the skillet, steam the cabbage about 5 minutes, add the broth, cover again, and simmer till the cabbage is very tender, about 15 minutes. Return the bacon to the skillet and toss well.

• Preheat the oven to 400°F. Grease a large, shallow baking dish.

• Combine the cabbage and bacon with the mashed potatoes in the mixing bowl, add the salt and pepper, and stir till well blended. Scrape the mixture into the prepared baking dish, dot the top with the remaining 3 tablespoons of butter cut into pieces, and bake till crusty brown, about 20 minutes. Serve hot.

MAKES 6 SERVINGS

BACON BONUS
Since some bacons are quite salty, always taste those cooked for salads, sandwiches, and breads before adding any salt.

russian creamed sauerkraut with bacon and shiitakes

Perhaps the reason Russian cooks take sauerkraut so seriously is because most still prepare their own at home—a tart, crunchy, full-flavored staple that is fermented at least a week in large bowls or buckets during the winter months. Although our sauerkraut is generally pale by comparison, what you find in barrels in some Russian or German delis is a good approximation, and packaged (not jarred) sauerkraut is respectable enough for this multiflavored dish. Be sure to use a good double-smoked bacon, and feel free to experiment with all types of wild mushrooms. This sauerkraut is delicious with virtually any pork dish.

6 ounces German *Speck* or double-smoked bacon (rind removed), diced
1 large onion, chopped
¼ pound shiitake mushrooms, chopped
2 pounds packaged sauerkraut, rinsed and drained
1 cup chicken broth
2 teaspoons caraway seeds
1 small dill pickle, minced
½ teaspoon sugar
¼ cup sour cream
Freshly ground black pepper to taste

• In a large casserole or Dutch oven, fry the bacon over moderate heat till it releases most of its fat, add the onion and mushrooms, and stir about 8 minutes. Add the sauerkraut, toss well, and stir about 5 minutes. Add the broth, caraway seeds, pickle, sugar, sour cream, and pepper and stir. Bring to a low boil, reduce the heat to low, cover, and simmer about 45 minutes. Serve hot.

MAKES 4 TO 6 SERVINGS

italian radicchio smothered with pancetta

Until about twenty years ago, the red-leafed Italian chicory called radicchio was virtually unknown in American markets and restaurants, so you can imagine my excitement when, in the town of Treviso, north of Venice, to research the origins of the creamy dessert tiramisù, I was first served the delectable leaves braised with spicy pancetta. Today, there are many styles and sizes of radicchio in our better food shops, but the least bitter and most flavorful variety is still, in my opinion, the same small, deep-purple Treviso heads with white ribs that I encountered on home ground many years ago. The prime season for radicchio is winter, and look for compact heads that have crisp, full-colored leaves with no brown spots. Suffice it to say that the combination of this slightly bitter vegetable and mellow pancetta is amazing.

4 heads radicchio (about 1 pound)
2 tablespoons olive oil
4 ounces pancetta, finely chopped
1 medium onion, finely chopped
1 small garlic clove, minced
Salt and freshly ground black pepper to taste
2 tablespoons dry vermouth

• Cut off and discard the root ends of the radicchio and discard any outer leaves that are wilted or discolored. Tear the leaves into 2 or 3 pieces and set aside.

• In a large skillet, heat the oil over moderate heat, add the pancetta, onion, garlic, and salt and pepper, and stir till the onion is golden, about 5 minutes. Add the vermouth and stir 1 minute longer. Add half the radicchio leaves, stir till they diminish in bulk, then add the remaining leaves and stir. Cover the pan, reduce the heat to low, and cook till the ribs are just tender, about 30 minutes. Uncover and, if there's any liquid left in the pan, increase the heat and boil till it has evaporated. Serve immediately.

MAKES 4 SERVINGS

chinese stir-fried greens and bacon

In China, air-dried bacon is used primarily to season any number of dishes, the most popular being stir-fried vegetables. For this particular stir-fry, do try to use bok choy, often sold in our markets as "Chinese white cabbage" or "white mustard cabbage" and easily identified by its cream-colored, thickly veined leaves and pale green tips. Because of their distinctive nutty flavors and high smoke points, peanut and sesame oils are ideal for stir-frying these greens. Be careful, however, for the oils—especially the sesame—can still burn if left over very high heat too long.

3 ounces air-cured Chinese bacon, soaked in water at least 6 hours (rind removed) and coarsely chopped
1 tablespoon peanut oil
1 tablespoon sesame oil
3 garlic cloves, peeled and finely sliced
2 teaspoons salt
2 pounds Chinese greens (bok choy, Savoy or Napa cabbage, or spinach), shredded
2 tablespoons chicken broth

• In a wok or large, heavy skillet, fry the bacon over moderate heat till crisp, drain on paper towels, and pour off all but 1 tablespoon of the fat. Add the two oils to the bacon fat, increase the heat to high, and when slightly smoking, add the garlic and salt and stir-fry for 15 seconds. Add the greens and stir-fry till wilted, 3 to 4 minutes. Add the broth and bacon and stir-fry till the greens are still slightly crisp, about 2 minutes. Serve immediately.

MAKES 4 SERVINGS

smoky hoppin' john

Traditionally served with a pork dish on New Year's Day for good luck, a dish of black-eyed peas simmered with vegetables, some form of bacon, and zesty seasonings has been called hoppin' John throughout the American South for as long as anybody can remember (though nobody has any idea how the name came about). Serious cooks wouldn't dream of preparing the dish with anything but fresh peas, though, actually, the frozen (but not canned) ones work just as well. Here you want to use a relatively lean hickory-smoked bacon, and when timing the cooking, remember that the peas should be neither al dente nor mushy but fully tender. Many Southerners like to serve their hoppin' John on top of boiled rice or topped with stewed tomatoes, but I find these accompaniments unnecessary if the peas are cooked to perfection. And if you want to follow local custom, be sure to serve small bowls of leftover cooking liquid ("pot likker") in which to dunk cornbread or any other style of bread you might serve.

¼ pound hickory-smoked bacon, cut into small pieces
1 small onion, finely chopped
1 celery rib, finely chopped
1 garlic clove, minced
2 pounds black-eyed peas (fresh or frozen and thawed)
Salt and freshly ground black pepper to taste
1 quart water

• In a large saucepan, fry the bacon over moderate heat till crisp and drain off all but 1 tablespoon of the fat. Add the onion, celery, and garlic and stir till softened, about 5 minutes. Add the remaining ingredients, bring to a boil, reduce the heat to low, cover, and simmer till the peas are tender but not mushy, about 1 hour. Serve hot.

MAKES 6 TO 8 SERVINGS

authentic boston baked beans with bacon

Originally prepared by Puritan Bostonian housewives on Saturday to be served both for dinner that night and the next day (cooking was forbidden on the Sabbath), authentic Boston baked beans are as rare in Boston today as the delectable steamed Boston brown bread once served with the beans. In fact, the only true Boston baked beans I've eaten in the past few years were served not in Boston but at a homey restaurant in Middlebury, Vermont. These didn't bear a scant resemblance to those canned tomatoey products seasoned more often than not with disgusting bits of processed frankfurters and not a hint of smoky bacon or molasses; and they were even altogether different in flavor and texture from the more respectable commercial beans that at least approximate the original. Adding a little rum to the long-simmering beans, of course, would have horrified the righteous Puritan ladies, but subsequent bean lovers learned many generations ago the advantage of this distinctive flavoring. These luscious beans are the best excuse I know to invest in a fine, two-quart earthenware bean pot.

4 cups dried pea beans (about 2 pounds)
1 teaspoon baking soda
1 medium onion, studded with 2 cloves
1 pound slab bacon (rind removed), cut into ¼-inch cubes
1½ cups dark molasses
2 teaspoons dry mustard
2 tablespoons salt
Freshly ground black pepper to taste
2 tablespoons dark rum

- Place the beans in a kettle with enough water to cover by 3 inches and soak overnight.
- Preheat the oven to 275°F.
- Drain the beans, add fresh water to cover by 1 inch, and add the baking soda and onion. Bring the beans to a low boil, simmer for 15 minutes, then transfer the contents of the kettle to a 2-quart bean pot or casserole. Add the bacon to the beans and combine thoroughly. Stir in the molasses, mustard, salt, pepper, and the rum, place the pot in the oven, and bake slowly till tender, 5 to 6 hours. Add a little water if necessary, but allow the top of the beans to crust slightly during the final 30 minutes of baking. Serve hot.

MAKES 6 TO 8 SERVINGS

english faggots and split peas

Despite the name's derogatory connotation in American English, faggots are one of the most respected and beloved dishes in England (especially in the rural northern shires). Traditionally made with a variety of pork offal along with plenty of bacon, herbs, and spices, the heady squares or balls are slowly baked till crispy and served either hot with mushy split peas and maybe applesauce or cold with salad. Since authentic faggots can be an acquired taste because of all the organ meats and fat, here I've limited the offal to a small amount of pig's liver and reduced the salt pork. I've also kept the peas intact instead of mashing them with butter the way English cooks do. If you love French *crépinettes,* you'll love these English faggots, and I know of no British dish that depends more on bacon for optimal success.

FOR THE FAGGOTS
8 ounces English or lean slab bacon (rind removed), cut into pieces
3 ounces lean salt pork
¼ pound pig's liver, cut into pieces
2 medium onions, quartered
2 cups chicken broth
½ cup soft bread crumbs
½ teaspoon dried thyme, crumbled
½ teaspoon powdered sage
¼ teaspoon ground nutmeg
Salt and freshly ground black pepper to taste

FOR THE PEAS
2 tablespoons ketchup
1 teaspoon tomato purée
1 teaspoon Worcestershire sauce
2 cups water
1 medium onion, quartered
12 ounces dried split peas
4 tablespoons (½ stick) butter
Salt and freshly ground black pepper to taste

• To make the faggots, combine the bacon, salt pork, liver, onions, and broth in a large saucepan, bring to a boil, reduce the heat to low, cover, and simmer for 45 minutes. Drain the meats and onion in a colander and reserve the cooking liquid.

• Preheat the oven to 375°F. Grease a shallow 2½-quart baking dish and set aside.

- In a food processor, mince the meats and onions and transfer to a mixing bowl. Add the bread crumbs, thyme, sage, nutmeg, and salt and pepper and, using your hands, combine till the mixture is well blended. Form the mixture into 8 balls, arrange them in the prepared baking dish, add 1½ cups of the reserved cooking liquid, and bake till slightly crispy on top, 45 to 50 minutes.

- Meanwhile, to cook the peas, combine the ketchup, tomato purée, Worcestershire, and water in a saucepan and whisk till well blended. Add the onion and bring to a boil. Add the peas, reduce the heat to low, cover, and simmer the peas till tender, about 30 minutes. Transfer to a serving bowl, add the butter and salt and pepper, and stir gently till the butter melts.

- Serve 2 faggots per person surrounded by equal portions of the peas.

MAKES 4 SERVINGS

BACON BUZZ
"Rasher" is the British term for a slice of streaky bacon. The expression was first used in the sixteenth century to distinguish an individual serving from the whole side of meat (or "flitch").

swiss apple, pear, potato, and bacon braise

Served throughout German-speaking Switzerland with all sorts of veal and game dishes, this hearty braise would be most often made with the mellow, beechwood-smoked bacon known as *Geräucherterspeck*. Of course, versions of the dish vary from region to region, but since Switzerland boasts such superior apple varieties as *Zapfenapfel* and *Grossmutterapfel*, and such luscious pears as the brown-skinned Kaiser Alexander and small *Eierbirnli*, it's not unusual for cooks to combine both fruits, as in this classic recipe. *Speck* is available in all of our German markets and delis (and in some upscale food shops), but if you must substitute slab bacon, just make sure that it's double-smoked.

One 10-ounce piece German *Speck* or double-smoked slab bacon (rind removed), cut into small chunks
2 tablespoons butter
1 large onion, chopped
1 cooking apple, peeled, cored, and sliced
1 firm bosc or seckel pear, peeled, cored, and sliced
1 tablespoon sugar
1 pound potatoes, peeled and roughly chopped
Salt and freshly ground black pepper to taste
2 tablespoons heavy cream

• In a large, heavy saucepan, fry the bacon over moderate heat till almost crisp and pour off all but about 2 tablespoons of the fat. Add the butter to the fat, add the onion, and stir till softened, about 5 minutes. Add the apple and pear, sprinkle the sugar over the top, and stir. Add the potatoes plus enough water to barely cover, bring to a low boil, reduce the heat to moderate, and simmer till most of the liquid has evaporated, about 30 minutes. Add the salt and pepper and cream, stir well, and let simmer about 5 minutes longer. Serve hot.

MAKES 4 TO 6 SERVINGS

swedish apples and onions with bacon

Apples, onions, and smoky bacon are one of the great culinary combinations throughout Scandinavia, and while any *äppel-fläsk* is deemed a peasant dish, this one from Skåne in Sweden couldn't be more perfect with roast pork for a casual Sunday supper. It's quick and easy to prepare, it can be served right in the skillet, and it's utterly delicious. Note that since Danish and English bacon tend to be quite salty, only a few grinds of the peppermill are needed for seasoning.

4 tablespoons (½ stick) butter
1 pound Danish or English bacon slices, diced
2 large onions, thinly sliced
2 red cooking apples, unpeeled, cored, and cut into thin wedges
Freshly ground black pepper to taste

• In a large, heavy skillet, melt 2 tablespoons of the butter over moderate heat, add the bacon, fry till lightly browned, about 8 minutes, and drain on paper towels.

• Melt the remaining 2 tablespoons of butter in the skillet, add the onions, and stir till softened, about 8 minutes. Add the apples, cover the pan, reduce the heat to low, and simmer till the apples are slightly soft, about 8 minutes, stirring to prevent sticking. Return the bacon to the onions and apples, stir, cover, and simmer till the bacon is heated through, 3 to 5 minutes longer. Season with pepper and serve directly from the pan.

MAKES 4 SERVINGS

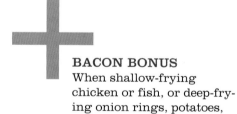

BACON BONUS
When shallow-frying chicken or fish, or deep-frying onion rings, potatoes, okra, and other vegetables, a tablespoon of bacon fat added to the cooking oil adds delectable flavor.

pasta and rice

Italian Spaghetti alla Carbonara

Swiss Macaroni, Bacon, and Cheese

French Noodles with Bacon, Tomatoes, and Basil

Hungarian Noodles with Bacon and Cottage Cheese

Italian Linguine with Shrimp, Jerusalem Artichokes,
and Bacon

Savannah Red Rice

Shrimp, Bacon, Egg, and Rice Strata

Caribbean Bacon, Cheese, and Rice Custard

English Bacon and Rice Pilaf

Chinese Pork Fried Rice with Bacon

Lowcountry Shrimp and Bacon Bog

Italian Fennel and Pancetta Risotto

Catalan Rice with Bacon, Raisins, and Pine Nuts

Chinese Sweet Rice with Black Mushrooms and Bacon

Minnesota Wild Rice with Bacon, Almonds,
and Oyster Mushrooms

italian spaghetti alla carbonara

Supposedly named after coal miners from Abruzzo who would come to Rome to sell their charcoal, *spaghetti alla carbonara* is surely Italy's most famous pasta dish and one that depends on spicy pancetta for much of its unique identity. Two cardinal sins often committed in the United States (even in Italian restaurants) are the addition of cream and the substitution of smoked bacon. Neither is authentic, and both destroy the concept of the original. As for the raw eggs and fear of salmonella, the hot spaghetti should cook the eggs and kill any possible bacteria, but if you're still squeamish, prepare another pasta dish. (Pasteurized eggs, of course, could be used, but the taste and texture of the dish will assuredly not be the same.)

1 tablespoon olive oil
6 ounces pancetta, diced
Salt to taste
1 pound dried spaghetti
3 large eggs, beaten
2 ounces Parmigiano-Reggiano cheese, grated
2 ounces Pecorino Romano cheese, grated
Freshly ground black pepper to taste

• In a medium skillet, heat the olive oil over moderate heat, add the pancetta, and fry till lightly browned, about 5 minutes. Keep warm over low heat.

• Bring a large kettle of salted water to a rolling boil, add the spaghetti, return to the boil, and cook till al dente, about 10 minutes. Drain off all the water from the kettle, add the eggs, the pancetta with its rendered fat, half of each cheese, and the pepper, and toss with 2 large forks till the eggs are completely incorporated and coat the spaghetti. (The heat of the spaghetti will cook the eggs.) Add the remaining cheeses, toss again till well incorporated, taste for salt and pepper, and serve immediately.

MAKES 4 SERVINGS

swiss macaroni, bacon, and cheese

When I first sampled this Swiss specialty in the Alps above Lucerne, it was prepared with half macaroni, half cubed potatoes, Emmentaler cheese, and a salty, rugged mountain bacon that tasted almost like country ham. Then, later, after visiting a Gruyère cheesemaker in the canton of Fribourg, some friends and I were treated to basically the same dish at a chalet-restaurant, the differences being that only macaroni was used, the smoky bacon was much like our streaky style, and, of course, the cheese was a buttery, nutty Gruyère. Topped with golden onions and served with only some cinnamon apple wedges sautéed in butter and a very tart green salad, it was one of the greatest pasta dishes I've ever encountered and almost made a mockery of ordinary mac 'n' cheese.

Salt to taste
1 pound dried elbow macaroni
6 ounces streaky bacon slices, cut into small pieces
4 tablespoons (½ stick) butter
1 cup heavy cream
Freshly ground black pepper to taste
Grated nutmeg to taste
4 ounces Gruyère or Emmentaler cheese, grated
1 medium onion, thinly sliced

• Bring a large kettle of salted water to a boil, add the macaroni, return to the boil, and cook till al dente, about 10 minutes. Drain.

• Preheat the oven to 350°F. Butter a 2- to 2½-quart baking dish and set aside.

• In a large, deep skillet, fry the bacon over moderate heat till almost crisp, drain off all but 1 tablespoon of fat, and add 2 tablespoons of the butter to the fat. Add the cream, pepper, and nutmeg and stir well. Add the cooked macaroni and the cheese and mix till well blended. Scrape the mixture into the prepared baking dish and bake till bubbly and golden, 10 to 15 minutes.

• Meanwhile, melt the remaining 2 tablespoons of butter over moderately low heat in a small skillet, add the onion, and cook till golden, about 5 minutes. Scatter the onions over the top of the macaroni and serve hot.

MAKES 4 SERVINGS

french noodles with bacon, tomatoes, and basil

Noodles are almost as popular along the southern coast of France as in Italy, the perfect accompaniment to the region's large variety of ragouts, daubes, navarins, and blanquettes. (And elsewhere in France, such classic stews as *boeuf bourguignon* and *civet de lapin* are traditionally served with some form of noodle.) Combined with *lardons* of fresh, unsmoked bacon called *poitrine fraîche* or with cured, unsmoked *ventrèche,* ripe chopped tomatoes, and fresh basil, this particular preparation goes well with not only simple meat stews but also roasted pork or thick pan-fried pork chops. If you can't find French bacon, use salt pork for the *lardons*—blanched, as directed, to release a little of the salt.

½ pound French unsmoked bacon, rind removed and the meat cut into *lardons* 1 inch long by ¼ inch thick
4 ripe medium tomatoes, peeled, seeded, and finely chopped
2 garlic cloves, minced
8 fresh basil leaves
Salt and freshly ground black pepper to taste
1 pound dried egg noodles
2 tablespoons chopped fresh parsley leaves

• Place the bacon in a saucepan with enough water to cover, bring to a boil, cook 3 minutes, drain, and pat dry with paper towels. In a small skillet, lightly brown the bacon over low heat, about 15 minutes, pour off half the fat, and keep the bacon and remaining fat warm.

• Place the tomatoes in a medium saucepan, add the garlic, basil, and salt and pepper, bring to a boil, and cook 5 minutes. Remove the basil leaves and keep the sauce warm.

• Bring a large kettle of salted water to a rolling boil, add the noodles, cook till al dente, about 10 minutes, and drain thoroughly. Pour the tomato sauce over the noodles, add the bacon plus its fat, toss well with a large fork, and taste for salt and pepper. Transfer the noodles to a wide serving bowl, sprinkle the top with parsley, and serve immediately.

MAKES 4 SERVINGS

hungarian noodles with bacon and cottage cheese

All you have to do to realize that Italy has no monopoly on noodles is make a tour of the restaurants of Budapest (simple and grand alike) and witness the many unusual noodle preparations. Of course most Hungarian cooks make their own egg noodles, and since so many of these farinaceous dishes depend on the country's unique styles of bacon for flavoring (paprika, gypsy, garlic, spiced, etc.), it's understandable that locals can often be seen making a meal of only noodles enriched with other components and maybe a tart green salad. Hungarian bacons are indeed special and can usually be found in the Middle European butcher shops and delis of our larger cities (or ordered on the Internet). Otherwise, use diced salt pork with streaks of lean for this dish. Do notice here that the bacon drippings are as important as the bacon itself.

¼ pound Hungarian paprika or garlic bacon (rind removed), cut into small dice
Salt to taste
1 pound dried noodles (medium egg noodles, tagliatelle, or fettuccine)
½ pound cottage cheese
Freshly ground black pepper to taste

• In a skillet, fry the bacon over moderate heat till crisp, drain on paper towels, and keep the drippings hot.

• Bring a large kettle of salted water to a rolling boil, add the noodles, return to the boil, and cook till tender, 10 to 12 minutes. Drain the noodles well, then add the bacon drippings, cottage cheese, and pepper and toss over very low heat to warm the cheese. Add the bacon, toss again, and serve immediately.

MAKES 6 SERVINGS

BACON BUZZ
Hungary boasts more than twenty different categories of bacon, and within each category several variations. In addition to ordinary smoked and paprika bacon are corn bacon, garlic bacon, rib bacon, gypsy bacon, and blood-coated bacon.

italian linguine with shrimp, jerusalem artichokes, and bacon

If you've never eaten Jerusalem artichokes (as opposed to the more ordinary globe variety), I can think of no better introduction than this northern Italian pasta specialty that contrasts the sweetness of shrimp with the slight earthiness of pine nuts and artichokes with the spiciness of pancetta. In truth, the Jerusalem artichoke (or, as it's often marketed in this country, sunchoke) has no connection whatsoever with Jerusalem, nor is it an artichoke. Rather, it is a tuber that derives its name from *girasole,* the Italian word for sunflower. Nut-brown and almost potato-flavored, the gnarled, twisted roots also grow wild in the eastern United States and are available in better markets over the winter months. Since they can be very awkward to peel, look for tubers that are firm and least gnarled. If you're unable to find Jerusalem artichokes, you can substitute about 2 cups of drained, thinly sliced bottled globe artichoke hearts.

½ pound Jerusalem artichokes (about 6)
½ pound pancetta, chopped
4 tablespoons (½ stick) butter
1 small onion, chopped
2 garlic cloves, minced
One 4-ounce jar pimentos, drained and chopped
¼ cup pine nuts
Salt and freshly ground black pepper to taste
Cayenne pepper to taste
½ pound fresh medium shrimp, shelled and deveined
½ pound finely chopped fresh parsley leaves
1 pound dried linguine

• Scrub the artichokes, cut away the eyes and small knobs, peel, slice thinly, and set aside.

• In a large skillet, fry the pancetta over moderate heat till lightly browned, about 5 minutes, and drain on paper towels. Pour off all but about 2 tablespoons of fat from the skillet and melt the butter in the bacon fat. Add the onion and garlic and stir for about 1 minute. Add the artichokes, pimentos, pine nuts, salt and pepper, and cayenne and stir the mixture about 5 minutes. Add the pancetta, shrimp, and parsley, stir, cover the skillet, and cook till the shrimp are fully pink, about 4 minutes. Remove from the heat and keep warm.

• Bring a large kettle of salted water to a rolling boil, add the linguine, return to the boil, and cook till al dente, about 10 minutes. Drain the linguine, divide it among serving plates or bowls, and spoon equal amounts of the shrimp mixture over each portion. Serve immediately.

MAKES 4 SERVINGS

savannah red rice

This classic staple of Savannah and the surrounding Georgia Lowcountry is red by virtue of the tomatoes, tomato purée, or tomato paste that is always used to give the rice a ruddy color and slightly tangy flavor. To make the rice without some form of bacon would be inconceivable, and on home ground the preferred variety is local country bacon produced from the same hogs raised for luscious country hams. Since this style of pungent, salty bacon is rarely available outside the South, the best substitute is one of the double-smoked slab bacons available from artisanal producers on the Internet and in many supermarkets. The texture of this rice should be fluffy and almost dry, and the best way to accomplish this is to stir it well with a fork about midway through cooking and again at the end till the grains are virtually separate. Serve this rice as you would any simple preparation of rice.

½ pound double-smoked sliced bacon
2 medium onions, finely chopped
6 ounces (1 small can) tomato paste
2 cups water
3 teaspoons salt
2 to 3 teaspoons sugar
Freshly ground black pepper to taste
Tabasco sauce to taste
2 cups long-grain rice

• In a large skillet, fry the bacon over moderate heat till crisp, drain on paper towels, and crumble. Pour off half the fat from the skillet and reserve.

• Add the onions to the fat in the skillet and stir for 2 minutes. Add the tomato paste, water, salt, sugar, pepper, and Tabasco, stir well, and let cook 10 minutes.

• Transfer the contents of the skillet to a large saucepan, add the reserved bacon fat, and bring to a boil. Add the rice, reduce the heat to moderately low, stir, cover, and cook till the rice has absorbed most of the liquid, 25 to 30 minutes. Remove the pan from the heat, add the crumbled bacon, stir well with a fork, and let the rice stand about 5 minutes to dry slightly. Fluff again with the fork and serve immediately.

MAKES 6 SERVINGS

shrimp, bacon, egg, and rice strata

To my mind, there's not a shrimp appetizer, salad, mousse, casserole, or stew that is not enhanced by a little bacon, and when it comes to ideal buffet dishes, this layered rice strata is hard to beat. Best of all, the dish can be assembled and chilled in advance without the top layer of tomatoes (which might make the rice too soggy), then finished off shortly before serving. Feel free to experiment with various smoked bacons.

1 cup water
½ cup long-grain rice
1 pound small fresh shrimp
6 slices hickory-smoked bacon
3 ripe medium tomatoes, peeled, seeded, and coarsely chopped
1 tablespoon Worcestershire sauce
Salt and freshly ground black pepper to taste
4 large hard-boiled eggs, sliced
1 cup dry bread crumbs
3 tablespoons butter, melted

• In a small saucepan, bring the water to a boil, add the rice, reduce the heat to a low simmer, cover, and cook for 15 minutes. Turn off the heat, let the rice stand for 10 minutes, fluff with a fork, and set aside.

• Meanwhile, combine the shrimp with enough water to cover in a medium saucepan, bring to a boil, and drain. When cool enough to handle, shell and devein the shrimp and set aside.

• In a medium skillet, fry the bacon over moderate heat till crisp, drain on paper towels, and crumble.

• Preheat the oven to 350°F. Butter a 2-quart baking dish and set aside.

• Spoon ⅔ of the tomatoes over the bottom of the prepared baking dish and arrange the shrimp evenly over the tomatoes. Layer the rice over the tomatoes, layer the egg slices over the rice, sprinkle the crumbled bacon over the eggs, and spoon the remaining tomatoes over the top.

• In a small bowl, toss the bread crumbs with the butter, spoon evenly over the top of the tomatoes, and bake till golden brown, about 25 minutes. Serve hot.

MAKES 6 SERVINGS

caribbean bacon, cheese, and rice custard

There are as many savory as sweet "custards" prepared throughout the Caribbean islands (plus in a few South American countries), and this one made with rice, smoky bacon, and the delectable cheese known as *queso blanco* is one of the most popular. Today, fresh *queso blanco* is often available in our finest cheese shops and some supermarkets (especially on the West Coast), but if you're unable to find it, a good substitute is Münster. In the Caribbean, this custard would be served with roasted or barbecued pig, goat, and other meats. And if you want to be authentic, bake the custard in an earthenware vessel.

8 slices streaky bacon
2 cups boiled rice
1 small onion, grated
2 ounces *queso blanco* cheese, shredded
1 tablespoon chopped fresh parsley leaves
1 large egg, beaten
2 tablespoons half-and-half
2 tablespoons butter, melted
¼ teaspoon sweet paprika
Salt and freshly ground black pepper to taste

• Preheat the oven to 325°F. Butter a 1½-quart casserole or baking dish and set aside.

• In a large skillet, fry the bacon over moderate heat till cooked but still slightly soft and drain on paper towels. Line the bottom and sides of the prepared casserole with the bacon slices.

• In a mixing bowl, combine all the remaining ingredients and stir till well blended. Scrape the mixture into the casserole, bake till the custard is set, about 30 minutes, and serve hot or warm.

MAKES 4 SERVINGS

english bacon and rice pilaf

No matter that it's ludicrous to call pilaf "rice pilaf," or that the Indian original usually involves curried white rice instead of brown, or that the rice should be lightly browned in butter instead of bacon drippings before being boiled instead of baked in broth. The English have had their own way of dealing with pilaf since the eighteenth century, and I'm the first to proclaim it utterly delicious most of the time—especially when served with a roasted game bird or lusty stew. Brown rice differs from white in that only the outer husk of the grain is removed, leaving a bran coating that accounts for both the tan color and delectably nutty flavor. If English or Irish bacon is unavailable, substitute regular streaky American bacon, and when seasoning the pilaf, remember that the foreign bacons tend to be considerably saltier than ours.

4 slices English or Irish bacon, cut into small dice
1 small onion, finely chopped
1 cup brown rice
2 cups chicken broth
Salt and freshly ground black pepper to taste

- Preheat the oven to 375°F.
- In a heavy medium casserole, fry the bacon over moderate heat till crisp and drain on paper towels. Add the onion to the drippings in the pot and stir till softened, about 3 minutes. Add the rice and stir till it softens and is well coated, about 5 minutes. Add the broth and salt and pepper, cover, and bake for 5 minutes. Reduce the heat to 350°F and continue baking till the rice has absorbed all the broth, 20 to 25 minutes. Add the bacon to the pilaf, toss quickly with a fork, and serve hot.

MAKES 4 SERVINGS

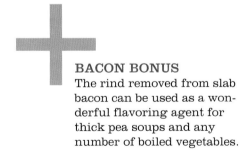

BACON BONUS
The rind removed from slab bacon can be used as a wonderful flavoring agent for thick pea soups and any number of boiled vegetables.

chinese pork fried rice with bacon

Of all the Chinese dishes that partly depend on air-dried bacon for their success, pork fried rice is by far my favorite. And if your only exposure to pork fried rice is the insipid concoction found in most Chinese takeouts, wait till you taste this authentic version that my Chinese culinary guru, Thom Chu, showed me how to prepare. Yes the prep work for all the ingredients is time-consuming, but once you've assembled everything, the actual stir-frying is a cinch. The rice is great with barbecued spareribs or chicken wings, but as Thom has pointed out, in China this is considered a one-dish meal made mostly from leftover rice and other ingredients that might be on hand. (If you happen to have a few peas or diced carrots in the refrigerator, feel free to toss those in also.) For stir-frying, the oil should be just shimmering and barely smoking, but remember that even peanut oil can burn if the heat's too high.

3 ounces air-dried Chinese bacon, soaked in water at least 6 hours
2 teaspoons soy sauce
2 teaspoons sesame oil
1 teaspoon dry sherry
1 teaspoon baking soda
1 teaspoon cornstarch
½ pound lean pork butt or shoulder, cut into small pieces
3 large eggs
1 teaspoon salt
¼ cup peanut oil
3 cups cooked long-grain rice, chilled
1 cup shredded iceberg lettuce
1 cup bean sprouts
¼ cup chopped scallions (part of green leaves included)

• Remove rind from the bacon, pat the meat dry, cut into ¼-inch-long sticks, and set aside.

• In a bowl, whisk together the soy sauce, 1 teaspoon of the sesame oil, and the sherry, baking soda, and cornstarch till well blended, add the pork, stir, and let marinate in the refrigerator about 1 hour.

• Meanwhile, fry the bacon in a small skillet over moderate heat till crisp and drain on paper towels.

• In another bowl, whisk together the eggs, the remaining teaspoon of sesame oil, and the salt till well blended and set aside.

• In a large wok or heavy 12-inch skillet, heat 2 tablespoons of the peanut oil over high heat till almost smoking, add the pork, stir-fry for 1 minute, and transfer to a plate. Add another tablespoon of oil to the pan, add the eggs, stir-fry quickly till just set, and transfer to the plate. Add another tablespoon of the oil to the pan, add the rice, and stir-fry for 5 minutes. Return the pork and eggs to the pan, add the bacon, lettuce, bean sprouts and scallions, and stir-fry the combination about 2 minutes longer. Serve immediately.

MAKES 4 SERVINGS

BACON BONUS
An acceptable substitute for Chinese bacon used to flavor many Chinese dishes is Smithfield or other country-cured ham.

lowcountry shrimp and bacon bog

Indigenous to the Carolina and Georgia coastal Lowcountry, a bog (unlike a fluffy perloo) is an almost soupy rice staple that is either prepared as a simple side dish or enriched with anything from seafood to chicken to country ham or smoked bacon and served as a main course. This luscious shrimp and bacon bog was once prepared at a friend's summer cottage on Sullivan's Island, near Charleston, and since then, I've considered it to be an ideal dish with which to experiment with all styles of premium bacon. Hickory-smoked slab bacon is what I use mostly, but one of the most memorable renditions was made with an artisanal peppered bacon from California I ordered on the Internet. Bogs are sometimes baked in the oven like perloos, but I've learned that the important texture of the rice can be much better controlled on top of the stove.

½ pound hickory-smoked sliced bacon, finely diced
2 medium onions, finely chopped
1½ cups long-grain rice, rinsed well and drained
2¼ cups chicken broth
2 ripe medium tomatoes, peeled, finely chopped, and juices retained
2 teaspoons fresh lemon juice
1½ teaspoons Worcestershire sauce
1 teaspoon salt
¼ teaspoon freshly ground black pepper
¼ teaspoon cayenne pepper
¼ teaspoon grated nutmeg
2 pounds fresh medium shrimp, shelled and deveined
¼ cup minced fresh parsley leaves

• In a large, heavy pot, fry the bacon over moderate heat till crisp, drain on paper towels, and set aside. Pour off all but about 3 tablespoons of fat from the pot, add the onions, and stir for 3 minutes. Add the rice and stir well. Add the broth, tomatoes with their juices, lemon juice, Worcestershire, salt, black pepper, cayenne, and nutmeg, bring to a low simmer, cover, and cook for 20 minutes. Stir in the bacon and the shrimp and continue cooking, uncovered, for 10 minutes, adding a little more broth if the rice seems to be drying out. Stir the bog with a fork, taste for seasoning, sprinkle the parsley on top, and serve immediately.

MAKES 6 SERVINGS

italian fennel and pancetta risotto

Just twenty years ago, it was difficult to find bulb fennel and Italian short-grain Arborio or Vialone rice in our markets and virtually impossible to buy spicy pancetta except in some Italian food shops. Today, all three are generally available in most reputable stores and supermarkets (now there is even domestic pancetta), making it possible for Americans to prepare an unusual risotto such as this one, which my friend John Mariani first told me about and that I later ate at a restaurant in Parma while on a trip researching Parmigiano-Reggiano cheese. I relish fresh fennel (which tastes of anise and just becomes sweeter when cooked), and when it's combined with pancetta and stirred slowly with the creamy rice, the result is sheer ecstasy. If pancetta is difficult to find, either lean salt pork or even prosciutto makes an acceptable substitution, but by no means try to substitute long-grain rice for the Arborio or Vialone since it will not produce the desired creaminess. As indicated, either chicken stock or broth can be used, but if you happen to have fresh, rich stock in the fridge, this is the time to use it. Do remember to be patient while cooking the rice, stirring it slowly and constantly till it is softly al dente or, to use the more correct Italian expression, *all'onda* (wavy).

1½ quarts fresh chicken stock or broth
3 tablespoons olive oil
3 tablespoons butter
1 small onion, minced
1 garlic clove, minced
¼ pound pancetta, finely diced
1 fresh medium fennel bulb, trimmed of discolored leaves and finely chopped
Salt and freshly ground black pepper to taste
2 cups Arborio or Vialone rice
½ cup dry white wine or vermouth
1 cup freshly grated Parmigiano-Reggiano cheese

- In a large saucepan, heat the chicken stock and keep it hot.
- In a medium flameproof casserole or heavy pot, heat the olive oil and 1 tablespoon of the butter over moderate heat, add the onion and garlic, and stir for 2 minutes. Add the pancetta and stir about 2 minutes or till lightly browned. Add the fennel and salt and pepper and stir about 3 minutes or till the fennel is softened.
- Add the rice and stir for 2 minutes to coat well. Add the wine, return the heat to moderate, and stir about 2 minutes or till the wine is absorbed. Add ½ cup of the hot chicken stock and stir till it is absorbed. Continue adding stock by the half cup, stirring and allowing the liquid to be absorbed till the rice is creamy but still al dente, about 20 minutes in all. Add the remaining 2 tablespoons of butter plus the cheese, stir well, adjust the salt and pepper to taste, and serve immediately.

MAKES 4 SERVINGS

catalan rice with bacon, raisins, and pine nuts

Contrary to popular perception in the United States, most of Spain's great rice dishes (paella included) are made with soft, creamy short-grain rice, and this luxurious Catalan specialty is no exception. Likewise, the carefully cured, unsmoked, delicately sweet Spanish bacon known as *tocino* is by far the most popular style used in cooking (smoked pig belly is simply referred to as "bacon"). Your best bet here is to use Italian Arborio or Vialone rice, and since it's still impossible in the United States to find genuine *tocino,* an appropriate substitute is either Italian pancetta or fine salt pork with just a trace of lean. The Spanish pine nuts (*pinyons*) that add such a wonderful crunch to this rice can be found packaged in specialty food shops and some supermarkets, but remember that because of their high fat content, the nuts turn rancid quickly if not stored airtight in the refrigerator (up to about 3 months).

3 ounces lean salt pork (rind removed), cut into small dice
6 tablespoons seedless dark raisins
¼ cup pine nuts
1½ cups short-grain rice
3 cups water
2 teaspoons salt

• In a large saucepan or pot, stir the salt pork over moderate heat till lightly browned, about 8 minutes, and drain on paper towels. Pour off all but about 2 tablespoons of the fat, reduce the heat slightly, add the raisins and pine nuts, and stir till the raisins plump and the nuts turn golden, about 5 minutes. Add the salt pork and rice, stir well, scraping any browned bits from the bottom of the pan, and set aside.

• In another pan, bring the water and salt to a boil. Return the pan with the rice to the heat, adding the boiling water, and cook the rice over low heat till all the liquid is absorbed, 20 to 25 minutes. Stir well and serve hot.

MAKES 4 SERVINGS

chinese sweet rice with black mushrooms and bacon

In China, glutinous short-grain rice is often called "sweet rice" because of the soft, mellow texture and taste, and when equally honeyed air-dried Chinese bacon is used to flavor the rice and other ingredients, the result is ambrosial. Look for Chinese black mushrooms in Asian markets and upscale supermarkets; if not available, substitute shiitakes. Here is a Chinese dish that requires lots of advance preparation of ingredients (a day ahead is best), but after you complete the stir-fry, the rice can easily be chilled till you're ready for the final steaming. Furthermore, the dish is almost as good when reheated over steaming water. Serve the rice with any baked or barbecued meat or poultry.

2 cups sweet rice (short-grain rice)
½ pound air-dried Chinese bacon, soaked at least 6 hours in water
½ cup Chinese black mushrooms
2 tablespoons peanut oil
½ cup finely chopped scallions (part of green leaves included)
1 tablespoon finely chopped fresh ginger
2 tablespoons coarsely chopped garlic
½ pound canned water chestnuts, sliced
2 cups chicken broth
2 tablespoons soy sauce
2 tablespoons dry sherry
Salt and freshly ground black pepper to taste

• Place the rice in a large bowl, cover with cold water, and soak overnight. Drain.

• Place the bacon in a large metal colander or strainer over gently boiling water in a pot, cover, and steam about 1 hour. Remove any rind and cut the meat into large dice.

• In a bowl, soak the mushrooms in warm water about 20 minutes, drain them and squeeze out the excess liquid, discard the stems, and coarsely chop the caps.

• In a wok or large, heavy skillet, heat the oil over high heat till almost smoking, add the scallions, ginger, and garlic, and stir-fry for 1 minute. Add the bacon, mushrooms, drained rice, and water chestnuts and continue to stir-fry for 3 minutes. Add the broth, soy sauce, sherry, and salt and pepper, reduce the heat to low, cover, and cook 15 minutes, stirring from time to time. Transfer the mixture to a heatproof bowl and cover with plastic wrap.

• Place a rack in a wok or large, deep saucepan and fill the vessel with 2 inches of water. Bring the water to a boil and lower the bowl with the mixture onto the rack. Reduce the heat to low, cover the vessel, and steam the mixture about 30 minutes. Serve immediately. (The rice can be reheated.)

MAKES 4 SERVINGS

minnesota wild rice with bacon, almonds, and oyster mushrooms

Wild rice is not a rice at all but rather a tall aquatic grass, and since Minnesota not only has more paddies under cultivation than any other state but can also boast some of the nation's finest artisanal bacon producers, it makes sense that the rice is often cooked with full-flavored bacon and other lusty ingredients as the ideal accompaniment to roast venison and pheasant, braised quail, and other popular game dishes. Wild rice must be rinsed thoroughly, and the best method is to place it in a bowl with cold water and swirl it with your fingers so that any debris will float to the surface. Remember also that if the rice is overcooked, it becomes gummy, so check after about 45 minutes of baking to make sure it's just tender.

2 thick slices cob-smoked bacon
1 medium onion, finely chopped
½ pound fresh oyster (or shiitake) mushrooms, washed, patted dry, and coarsely chopped
1 cup wild rice, washed thoroughly
2 cups chicken broth
½ teaspoon salt
¼ cup chopped toasted almonds
Freshly ground black pepper to taste

• Preheat the oven to 325°F.

• In a 2-quart flameproof casserole, fry the bacon over moderate heat till crisp, drain on paper towels, and crumble. Add the onion and mushrooms to the fat in the casserole and stir till softened, about 5 minutes. Add the wild rice and stir till well coated. Add the broth and salt and bring to a boil, stirring. Cover the casserole, place in the oven, and bake till the rice is tender but not gummy, about 50 minutes. Remove from the oven and let rest about 10 minutes. Add the bacon, almonds, and pepper, toss till well blended, and serve immediately.

MAKES 4 SERVINGS

BACON BUZZ
The first pigs in America were brought to Florida by Hernando de Soto in 1542.

breads

english bacon and cheddar bread

Found at old-fashioned restaurants and inns throughout the English countryside, this sublime bread is leavened with both baking powder and lard and is just as good at room temperature as piping hot from the oven. If you're unable to find English or Irish bacon, use a lean, hickory-smoked streaky one, and if you want to produce a truly exceptional bread, find a cheese shop (or serious supermarket) that stocks an aged farmhouse English cheddar or double Gloucester. I love to serve this bread with all types of soups and simple stews. Note that the bread keeps in the refrigerator up to a week and also freezes well wrapped tightly in foil.

½ pound English or Irish bacon, chopped
2½ cups all-purpose flour
1½ teaspoons baking powder
1 teaspoon salt
1 cup finely grated extra-sharp cheddar cheese
¼ cup lard, softened
2 tablespoons sugar
2 large eggs, beaten
1¼ cups milk
1 teaspoon Worcestershire sauce

• Preheat the oven to 350°F. Grease a 9½-by-5½-by-2½-inch loaf pan and set aside.

• In a skillet, fry the bacon over moderate heat till crisp and drain on paper towels.

• In a bowl, combine the flour, baking powder, and salt and stir till well blended. Add the cheese and toss well. In another large bowl, combine the lard and sugar and stir with a wooden spoon till blended. Add the eggs, milk, and Worcestershire and stir till blended. Add the flour mixture and bacon and stir just till the batter is well blended.

• Scrape the batter into the prepared loaf pan and bake till a knife inserted in the center comes out clean, about 45 minutes. Let the loaf cool 10 minutes in the pan, loosen the edges with the knife, and let cool completely on a rack.

MAKES 1 LOAF

german bacon pumpernickel bread

Germany's Baden region is renowned for the succulent hams and bacon produced on small mountain farms in the Black Forest, and while I must have eaten the local *Speck* in at least a dozen dishes during my many visits to Baden-Baden, the bacon pumpernickel bread served at a homey, dark-paneled inn about five miles above the city made a particularly indelible impression. Unlike most pumpernickels, this one was almost light in texture, no doubt the result of both plenty of yeast and white flour plus shortening. (Normally, a little baking soda should be added to a bread such as this to neutralize the acid in the molasses; here it's not needed.) Genuine Black Forest *Speck* is usually available in our German markets or online, but if you can't find it, be sure to substitute a double-smoked bacon.

2 envelopes active dry yeast
1 cup lukewarm water
¼ cup dark molasses
1 tablespoon vegetable shortening, softened
1 tablespoon salt
1 tablespoon caraway seeds
2 cups rye flour
1½ cups all-purpose flour
¼ pound Black Forest *Speck* or double-smoked bacon (rind removed), diced
Cornmeal

• In a small bowl, sprinkle the yeast over ½ cup of the water and let proof till bubbly, 5 to 10 minutes.

• In a large mixing bowl, combine the remaining ½ cup of water, molasses, shortening, salt, caraway seeds, and yeast mixture and beat with a wooden spoon till smooth. Gradually beat in the rye flour, then the all-purpose flour, and stir to make a soft dough. Transfer to a floured surface, knead about 5 minutes, and grease the mixing bowl. Form the dough into a ball, return it to the bowl, cover with plastic wrap, and let rise in a warm area till doubled in bulk, about 2 hours.

• In a skillet, fry the *Speck* over moderate heat till crisp and drain on paper towels. Grease a large baking sheet and sprinkle with cornmeal.

• Punch down the dough, transfer to a floured surface, add the *Speck,* and knead just till the bacon is well distributed. Form the dough into a slightly flattened oval, place on the prepared baking sheet, and, with a sharp knife, cut two 1-inch-deep slits in the top. Cover with plastic wrap and let rise again till doubled in bulk, about 1 hour.

• Preheat the oven to 350°F.

• Bake the loaf till browned and crusty, about 45 minutes, and transfer to a rack to cool.

MAKES 1 LARGE LOAF

sardinian bacon bread

For centuries, bread has been a symbol of family unity in Sardinia, and the open markets of Palermo and Messina are overflowing with every style of rugged country loaf, meat- or pecorino-cheese-stuffed rolls, crisp flat bread, and spiced biscuit imaginable. Perhaps most distinctive of all is this yeasty, crusty pancetta bread with the characteristic wide hole in the center, a truly sumptuous creation that is made either as a single large loaf or smaller individual ones. For the right texture, you must begin with a yeast sponge, and remember that it's important to widen the hole again with your fingers after the dough has risen the second time.

1 envelope active dry yeast
1 tablespoon sugar
2 cups lukewarm water
3½ cups all-purpose flour
½ pound pancetta, diced
2 teaspoons salt
1 teaspoon freshly ground black pepper

• In a large mixing bowl, combine the yeast, sugar, and 1 cup of the water and let proof about 5 minutes. Add 1 cup of the flour, beat vigorously with a wooden spoon till well blended, cover with plastic wrap, and let stand 2 hours.

• Meanwhile, fry the pancetta in a skillet over moderate heat till lightly browned, drain on paper towels, and reserve the fat.

• Add the remaining 1 cup of water, the salt, pepper, pancetta with its fat, and the remaining 2½ cups of flour to the yeast sponge and beat vigorously till the dough is very soft, adding a little more flour if the dough is too sticky. Cover with plastic wrap and let rise in a warm area till doubled in bulk, about 2 hours.

• Preheat the oven to 425°F. Grease a large baking sheet with olive oil and set aside.

• Transfer the dough to a floured surface and knead about 2 minutes. Form the dough into a smooth ball, flatten slightly, place on the prepared baking sheet, and, using your floured fingers, pull the dough outward from the center to form a wide hole in the center. Cover with plastic wrap and let rise about 30 minutes.

• Gently re-form the wide hole, bake the bread till golden and crusty, 35 to 40 minutes, and transfer to a rack to cool.

MAKES 1 LARGE LOAF

iowa bacon and onion casserole bread

Liz Clark's cooking school in Keokuk, Iowa, is known throughout the Midwest, and when Liz first gave me the recipe for this unusual bread, it was flavored only with leftover bacon fat collected in a coffee can. With my passion for bacon, I couldn't eventually resist adding a little of the meat itself to the dough, and the result was phenomenal. Feel free to use various styles of bacon, and if the bacon does not render enough fat to get you through the recipe, substitute a little melted vegetable shortening.

3 to 4 slices cob-smoked bacon, chopped
1 envelope active dry yeast
1½ cups lukewarm water
2 tablespoons sugar
2 teaspoons salt
4 to 5 cups unbleached bread flour, as needed
1 medium onion, finely diced
Cornmeal

• In a skillet, fry the bacon over moderate heat till crisp, drain on paper towels, and reserve the bacon fat.

• In a large mixing bowl, sprinkle the yeast over ½ cup of the water and let dissolve. Add the sugar, salt, the remaining 1 cup water, and 1½ cups of the flour and beat with an electric mixer till smooth, about 2 minutes. Set aside.

• In a small skillet, heat about 1 tablespoon of the bacon fat over moderate heat, add the onion, stir till softened, about 3 minutes, and remove from the heat.

• Add 2½ cups of the flour, the bacon, 1 tablespoon of the bacon fat, and the onion to the dough in the mixing bowl and stir till well blended, adding more flour as necessary to make a soft dough. Transfer the dough to a floured surface, knead till spongy, about 5 minutes, and form into a ball. Place the ball in a greased bowl, cover with plastic wrap, and let rise in a warm area till doubled in bulk, about 45 to 50 minutes.

• Preheat the oven to 400°F. Coat the inside surfaces of a deep round or oval 2½-quart casserole with a little of the bacon fat and sprinkle the surfaces with cornmeal to coat completely.

• Transfer the risen dough to the prepared casserole, cover with plastic wrap, and let rise again for about 20 minutes. Place the casserole on the center rack of the oven and bake till the bread sounds hollow when thumped, about 40 minutes. Brush the top with a little bacon grease, then transfer to a rack to cool. Serve the bread warm or at room temperature in wedges or slices.

MAKES 1 LARGE LOAF

castilian bacon-and-sausage-stuffed bread

Castile, in central Spain, is known not only for its once-majestic castles but also for its superior bacon and chorizo sausage, roasted meats, and, without question, the finest breads in the entire country. This stuffed bread (*hornago*) is typically served at Easter with various egg dishes, and I once had a version in Segovia that also included wedges of hard-boiled eggs stuffed in with the meats. Castilians seem to love the combination of smoky bacon and spicy sausage, and another similar specialty involves both meats encased in small dough rolls that are brushed with egg, baked till golden, and eaten as an appetizer or snack. Today, chorizo is found in all better markets and many delis.

1 envelope active dry yeast
1½ cups lukewarm water
3½ cups unbleached all-purpose flour
3 teaspoons salt
2 tablespoons olive oil
½ pound lean slab bacon (rind removed), diced
2 chorizo sausages, cut in quarters crosswise
Cornmeal

- In a small bowl, sprinkle the yeast over the water, stir, and let proof 5 to 10 minutes.
- In a large mixing bowl, combine the flour and salt, add the yeast mixture, and stir with a wooden spoon till the dough is just mixed. Transfer to a lightly floured surface and knead till the dough is elastic, about 10 minutes, adding more flour if necessary. Form the dough into a ball, place in an oiled bowl, turn to coat the dough with oil, cover with plastic wrap, and let rise in a warm area till doubled in bulk, about 2 hours.
- Shortly before the dough has finished rising, heat the olive oil in a skillet over moderate heat, add the bacon and sausage, cook about 10 minutes, turning, and drain on paper towels, reserving the fat.
- Punch the dough down, transfer to a floured surface, and knead in about 3 tablespoons of fat from the skillet. Shape into a ball, make slits in the sides with a knife, fill the slits with pieces of bacon and sausage, and close the dough well over the pieces. Sprinkle a heavy baking sheet with cornmeal, place the filled dough on the sheet, flatten slightly, cover with plastic wrap, and let rise again till doubled in bulk, about 1 hour.
- Preheat the oven to 425°F and place a small pan of boiling water on the bottom rack of the oven.
- Bake the loaf in the center of the oven 10 minutes, remove the pan of water, and continue baking till well browned, about 20 minutes longer. Serve the bread hot or warm in rough slices.

MAKES 1 LARGE LOAF

french provençal bacon flat bread

Except for the characteristic large openings throughout the bread, the yeasty *fougasse* baked in southern France is very similar in taste and texture to Italian focaccia. Along the Riviera, I've had this flat bread flavored with nuts, olives, herbs, and anchovies, but my favorite by far is the version studded with *lardons* made with either smoky *lard fumé* or salty *lard salé*. The best equivalent to these distinctive bacons is a smoked or unsmoked artisanal slab bacon, though I have made delicious *fougasse* with ordinary supermarket products. The bread can be served with virtually any dish, but my idea of ecstasy is to tear off shreds with my fingers while consuming a *salade niçoise* or other elaborate salad.

1 envelope active dry yeast
1 cup lukewarm water
3 cups all-purpose flour
1 tablespoon salt
½ pound slab bacon (rind removed), diced
1 large egg yolk, beaten

- In a small bowl, sprinkle the yeast over the water and let proof 5 to 10 minutes.
- In a large mixing bowl, combine the flour and salt and stir till well blended. Add the yeast mixture to the flour and stir slowly with a wooden spoon till the dough is slightly spongy, about 12 minutes, adding a little more flour if it becomes too sticky. Form the dough into a ball, cover the bowl with plastic wrap, and let rise in a warm area till doubled in bulk, about 2 hours.
- In a skillet, fry the bacon over moderate heat till almost crisp and drain on paper towels, reserving the fat.
- Grease 2 baking sheets with a little of the bacon fat (or with olive oil) and set aside.
- Add the bacon to the risen dough and knead till evenly incorporated. Cut the dough into 2 equal pieces, place each on a prepared baking sheet, and press each down to ovals about ½ inch thick. With a sharp knife, make 6 slits about 2 inches long in each oval and, with your fingers, separate the slits so you can see the pan below, stretching the dough out at the same time. Cover the ovals with plastic wrap and let rise again till doubled in bulk, 1 to 1½ hours.
- Preheat the oven to 450°F.
- If necessary, separate the slits in the dough again with your fingers, brush each flat bread with egg yolk, and bake in the center of the oven till golden brown, about 20 minutes. Serve warm.

MAKES 2 WIDE FLAT BREADS

italian bacon and onion flat bread

Thick like pizza crust, focaccia is Italy's puffy, versatile yeast bread that is often topped with everything from sautéed onions and bell peppers to boiled chickpeas to tangy grated cheeses, or studded with various types of meats, herbs, or even coarse salt. The tradition in Bologna is to enrich the flat bread with spicy pancetta and onions, and while it can certainly be served with meals, the bread is most often eaten as a snack or taken on picnics. Impractical as it can be to serve this bread straight from the oven, any piping hot focaccia is a real treat.

1 envelope active dry yeast
1 cup lukewarm water
3 cups all-purpose flour
1 tablespoon salt
3 tablespoons olive oil
¼ pound pancetta, diced
1 medium onion, finely chopped

- In a small bowl, sprinkle the yeast over ½ cup of the water, stir, and let proof 5 to 10 minutes.
- In a large mixing bowl, combine the flour and salt and stir till well blended. Add the remaining water, 2 tablespoons of the oil, and the yeast mixture and stir with a wooden spoon till the dough is almost sticky, adding a little more water if necessary. Transfer to a lightly floured surface and knead the dough till slightly spongy, about 5 minutes. Form the dough into a ball, return it to the bowl, cover with plastic wrap, and let rise in a warm area till doubled in bulk, about 2 hours.
- In a skillet, fry the pancetta over moderate heat till browned and drain on paper towels. Add the onion to the fat, stir till golden, about 5 minutes, and add to the pancetta.
- Grease an 8-by-12-inch baking pan and set aside.
- Punch down the dough in the bowl, add the pancetta and onion, and stir till well blended. Transfer to a floured surface, knead about 5 minutes, place on the prepared pan, and stretch the dough out to almost fill the pan. Brush with the remaining oil, cover with plastic wrap, and let rise about 30 minutes.
- Preheat the oven to 425°F.
- Bake the flat bread till golden brown, 20 to 25 minutes, transfer to a rack to cool slightly, and serve warm or at room temperature.

MAKES 1 LARGE FLAT BREAD

peppered-bacon cornbread

Throughout the American South, nothing is more loved and respected than cornbread studded with cracklings (crunchy pieces of rendered salt pork), but move elsewhere in the country and what you often find on home tables (though rarely in restaurants) is cornbread flavored with any number of regional bacons. I've eaten cornbread enhanced by cob-smoked bacon, garlic bacon, and honey-cured bacon, but one of the most memorable was this crusty peppered-bacon example whipped up by friends at a lobster roast I attended on the coast of Maine. People do tend to eat lots of buttered cornbread, but since it doesn't freeze at all well, make no more than you plan to serve—or possibly to use in place of bread crumbs.

4 to 5 lean slices peppered bacon, diced
4 cups yellow cornmeal
4 teaspoons baking powder
1 teaspoon salt
4 large eggs, beaten
4 cups milk
¼ cup vegetable oil

- In a skillet, fry the bacon over moderate heat till crisp and drain on paper towels.
- Preheat the oven to 425°F. Grease a 12-by-8-by-2-inch baking pan and set aside.
- In a large mixing bowl, combine the cornmeal, baking powder, and salt and stir well. Add the eggs, milk, and oil and stir with a wooden spoon till the batter is well blended and smooth. Add the bacon and stir till well distributed. Scrape the batter into the prepared pan and bake till a knife inserted in the center comes out clean, 25 to 30 minutes. Cut the cornbread into squares and serve hot with plenty of butter.

MAKES AT LEAST 8 SERVINGS

BACON BANTER
"Tom McNulty's [sheriff of Baltimore] specialty was made by spearing a slice of bacon on a large fork, jamming a soft crab down on it, holding the two over a charcoal brazier until the bacon had melted over the crab, and then slapping both upon a slice of hot toast."
—H. L. MENCKEN, *HAPPY DAYS,* 1940

portuguese bacon cornbread

My first exposure to northern Portugal's chewy, crusty cornbread known as *broa* was when I visited the region to learn about the production of Port wine, an occasion that also included my introduction also to the area's luscious, nutty, smoked bacon called *toucinho*. Although Portuguese bacon is still not available in the United States, I've learned that any lean, lightly smoked, artisanal slab bacon serves as a very credible substitute. Likewise, while most professional Portuguese bakers would bake this bread in steamy brick ovens to produce a dense crust, I've gotten pretty good results by merely placing a pan of boiling water on the lowest rack in the oven.

- 1 envelope active dry yeast
- 1 teaspoon sugar
- 2 cups lukewarm water
- 2 cups finely ground yellow cornmeal
- 2 teaspoons salt
- 1 tablespoon olive oil
- 1 cup lukewarm milk
- 3 cups sifted all-purpose flour
- ¼ pound lean slab bacon (rind removed), finely chopped

• In a small bowl, combine the yeast and sugar with ½ cup of the water and let proof till very bubbly, about 10 minutes.

• In a large mixing bowl, combine the cornmeal, salt, oil, milk, and remaining 1½ cups of water and stir till well blended. Add the yeast mixture, stir, then gradually add the flour and stir to make a soft dough. Transfer to a floured surface, knead till smooth, about 5 minutes, and grease the mixing bowl. Form the dough into a ball, return it to the bowl, cover with plastic wrap, and let rise in a warm area till doubled in bulk, about 1½ hours.

• In a skillet, fry the bacon till crisp and drain on paper towels, reserving about 1 tablespoon of the fat. Grease a 9-inch baking pan and set aside.

• Punch down the dough and transfer to a floured surface. Add the bacon plus the fat, knead to distribute the bacon evenly, about 5 minutes, and form the dough into an oval loaf. Place the loaf on the prepared baking sheet, cover with plastic wrap, and let rise in a warm area till doubled in bulk, about 1 hour.

• Preheat the oven to 450°F and place a pan of boiling water on the lowest rack.

• Bake the loaf in the center of the oven till browned and crusty, about 40 minutes, and transfer to a rack to cool.

MAKES 1 LOAF

southern bacon cornsticks

In the American South, various forms of bacon have been used for centuries to flavor biscuits, cornbread, hoecakes, hush puppies, muffins, and numerous other types of bread, and so beloved are cornsticks that some wizard even invented a special seven-compartment cast-iron mold in which to bake them. For these sticks to come out appropriately soft on the inside with crisp tops, the molds must be preheated till scorching hot and the cornsticks cooked at a high temperature. Although some Southerners can eat cornsticks warm or even cold, there's really nothing like a piping hot golden beauty smeared with plenty of butter.

4 lean slices hickory-smoked streaky bacon
1 cup yellow cornmeal
½ cup all-purpose flour
2 teaspoons sugar
2 teaspoons baking powder
½ teaspoon baking soda
½ teaspoon salt
1 large egg, beaten
½ cup buttermilk
2 tablespoons vegetable shortening, cut into bits and at room temperature

• In a skillet, fry the bacon over moderate heat till crisp, drain on paper towels, and finely crumble, reserving the fat.

• In a large mixing bowl, whisk together the cornmeal, flour, sugar, baking powder, baking soda, and salt till well blended. Add the egg and buttermilk and stir till well blended. Add the shortening and bacon, stir till well blended, cover the bowl with plastic wrap, and chill the batter for 1 hour.

• Preheat the oven to 475°F.

• Grease a 7-stick cast-iron cornstick mold with some of the bacon fat and place in the oven till very hot, about 5 minutes. Spoon the batter into the mold and bake till the tops are golden brown and crisp, 10 to 12 minutes. Serve piping hot.

MAKES SEVEN 5-INCH CORNSTICKS

bacon-parmesan biscuits

I've been tampering with these delectable biscuits for years, changing the size to accommodate the occasion, experimenting with new bacons and cheeses, and even using lard instead of vegetable shortening from time to time to make them crispier. Cut out with a 1-inch biscuit cutter, the biscuits are the perfect size for cocktail parties. They're also great for picnics, and nothing goes better with soups and elaborate salads. To ensure lightness, just remember to handle the dough as little as possible, and always watch the biscuits while they're baking to make sure they don't overbrown.

½ pound lean applewood-smoked bacon slices
2 cups all-purpose flour
1 tablespoon baking powder
½ teaspoon salt
Cayenne pepper to taste
⅓ cup chilled vegetable shortening
1 cup freshly grated Parmigiano-Reggiano cheese
1 cup milk

- In a large skillet, fry the bacon over moderate heat till crisp, drain on paper towels, and crumble finely.
- Preheat the oven to 425°F. Lightly grease a large baking sheet and set aside.
- In a large mixing bowl, whisk together the flour, baking powder, salt, and cayenne. Add the shortening and cut it into the flour with a pastry cutter, till the mixture is mealy. Add the bacon, cheese, and milk and stir just till the dry ingredients are well moistened.
- Transfer the dough to a lightly floured surface and knead 4 to 5 times—no more. Pat out the dough about ½ inch thick and cut out rounds with a 2-inch biscuit cutter. Pat the scraps together and cut out more rounds. Arrange the rounds on the prepared baking sheet about ½ inch apart and bake in the upper third of the oven till golden, 12 to 15 minutes. Let cool and store in an airtight container for up to 2 weeks.

MAKES ABOUT 1½ DOZEN BISCUITS

new england bacon yeast biscuits

Often called "angel" biscuits in New England because they're so light and fluffy, these yeast biscuits can be flavored with either diced salt pork that is rendered till crisp or one of the region's delectable maple- or cob-smoked bacons. Most supermarkets today carry at least one reliable brand of maple-smoked bacon, but if you're not satisfied with the looks of the package, order a premium artisanal product online. Be very careful not to stir this dough too much or knead it more than four or five times; otherwise, the biscuits will not rise fully when baked or could be tough.

3 slices lean maple-smoked bacon, finely diced
½ envelope active dry yeast
2 tablespoons lukewarm water
2 cups all-purpose flour
1 teaspoon baking powder
½ teaspoon salt
¼ cup vegetable shortening
1 cup milk

- In a skillet, fry the bacon over moderate heat till crisp and drain on paper towels.
- In a small bowl, sprinkle the yeast over the water and let proof till bubbly, 5 to 10 minutes.
- In a large mixing bowl, combine the flour, baking powder, and salt and whisk till well blended. Add the shortening and cut it into the flour with a pastry cutter or 2 knives till the mixture is mealy. Add the bacon and stir till well blended. Make a well in the dry ingredients, pour the yeast mixture and milk into the well, and stir gently with a wooden spoon just till the dry ingredients are moistened and the dough is soft. (Do not overmix.) Cover with plastic wrap and let rise in a warm area about 1 hour.
- Preheat the oven to 425°F.
- Transfer the dough to a floured surface and knead 3 or 4 times. Roll out the dough ½ inch thick and cut out rounds with a 2-inch biscuit cutter. Gather up the scraps of dough and repeat the procedure. Place the rounds on an ungreased baking sheet and bake in the upper third of the oven till golden brown, about 15 minutes.

MAKES AT LEAST 1 DOZEN BISCUITS

california bacon muffins

While the friend in San Francisco who introduced me to these sapid muffins wouldn't dream of using any bacon but the superior applewood-smoked version produced at Niman Ranch over in Oakland, I must admit that I've gotten just as good results with the ordinary hickory- or maple-smoked bacon found in most supermarkets. I don't like muffins too sweet, but if you, like Californians, do, by all means add a little more sugar to the batter. Do note that if you beat this batter too much, your muffins could be tough.

4 slices lean streaky bacon
2 cups all-purpose flour
2 tablespoons sugar
1 tablespoon baking powder
½ teaspoon salt
1 cup milk
2 large eggs, beaten
8 tablespoons (1 stick) butter, melted and cooled

• Preheat the oven to 400°F. Grease a standard 12-cup muffin tin and set aside.
• In a skillet, fry the bacon till crisp, drain on paper towels, and crumble finely.
• Into a large mixing bowl, sift together the flour, sugar, baking powder, and salt, add the bacon, and stir till well blended.
• In another bowl, whisk together the milk, eggs, and butter till well blended, add to the dry ingredients, and stir just till the flour is moistened. (Do not beat the batter.) Spoon the batter into the prepared muffin tin, filling the cups about two-thirds full, bake the muffins till golden, about 20 minutes, and serve hot.

MAKES 1 DOZEN 2½- TO 3-INCH MUFFINS

bacon, chive, and bell pepper scones

Throughout Britain, scones are almost exclusively a sweet bread spread with butter and fruit preserves for breakfast or afternoon teas, but in New England and the Upper Midwest of the United States, it's never unusual for home cooks to prepare savory scones flavored with everything from onions to cheese to bacon or ham and to serve them with soups and stews. The secret to these (or any) flaky scones is to handle the dough just as little as possible and knead it no more than eight or nine times. I love to make them with assertive cob-smoked bacon, but feel free to experiment with other styles.

3 slices cob-smoked bacon
½ medium green bell pepper, seeded and minced
2 cups all-purpose flour
1 tablespoon baking powder
½ teaspoon salt
Freshly ground black pepper to taste
¼ cup chilled lard, cut into bits
2 tablespoons minced chives
1 cup milk
1 large egg
1 teaspoon water

• In a skillet, fry the bacon over moderate heat till crisp, drain on paper towels, and crumble finely. Add the bell pepper to the skillet, stir till softened, about 5 minutes, and drain on paper towels.

• Preheat the oven to 425°F. Grease a large baking sheet and set aside.

• In a large mixing bowl, whisk together the flour, baking powder, salt, and pepper, add the lard, and work it with your fingertips till the mixture is crumbly. Add the bacon, bell pepper, and chives and stir till well blended. Add the milk and stir just till a sticky dough forms.

• Transfer the dough to a lightly floured surface, knead 8 to 9 times, and pat into a rectangle ¾ inch thick. With a sharp knife, cut the rectangle in half lengthwise and cut each half crosswise into 6 long, narrow triangles. Arrange the triangles on the prepared baking sheet about 1 inch apart.

• In a small bowl, whisk together the egg and water, brush the tops of the triangles lightly with the mixture, and bake in the center of the oven till just golden, 12 to 15 minutes. Serve hot.

MAKES 1 DOZEN SCONES

desserts

Corned bacon, 11
Cornsticks, Southern Bacon, 247
Cottage Cheese and Bacon, Hungarian Noodles with, 219
Couenne, 8
Country-style bacon, 5
Crab:
    Chowder, Maryland Shrimp, Bacon and, 78
    Legs, Bacon-Wrapped Dungeness, 37
Cracklings, Southern Shrimp and Pea Salad with, 104
Cream Cheese, Bacon, and Horseradish Dip, 30
Creamed Sauerkraut with Bacon and Shiitakes, Russian, 202
Cremini Mushrooms, Bacon-Stuffed, 35
Creole Shrimp, Louisiana, 178
Criollo, 95
Croques-Monsieur, Canadian Bacon, 114
Cunningham, Marion, 67
Cured bacon, 1, 2
Curing bacon, 3–4
Currants, Black, Burgundian Carrots with Onions, Bacon and, 193
Custard:
    Canadian Bacon Maple, 262
    Caribbean Bacon, Cheese, and Rice, 224

d

Danish bacon, 11
    cooking with, 58
    production of, 56
    purchasing, 12
Danish Potato, Tomato, and Bacon Omelette, 56
D'Artagnan, 17
Date Tapas, Grilled Bacon-Wrapped, 41
Denmark, styles of bacon in, 11
Devils on Horseback, 40
Dip:
    Bacon, Cream Cheese, and Horseradish, 30
    Hot Bacon—Blue Cheese, 31
Double-smoked bacon, 5
Dressing:
    Bacon, Blue Cheese, and Buttermilk, Iceberg Wedges with, 101
    Bacon, Chicken, Avocado, and Orange Salad with, 106
    Warm Bacon, Wilted Spinach and Avocado Salad with, 100
Dry-cured bacon, 3

Duck, Bacon, and Pinto Bean Stew, 128
Duck Gizzard, Cabbage, and Bacon Soup, French, 84–85

e

Ecuadorian Smoky Pumpkin Soup, 96
Edamame and Bacon Soup, Chilled, 76
Egg(s):
    Cake, Scandinavian Bacon and, 58
    California Hangtown Fry, 68
    Hash and, Russian, 70
    Omelette, Danish Potato, Tomato, and Bacon, 56
    Omelette, Italian Open-Face Zucchini and Bacon, 61
    Pie, English Bacon and, 55
    Pudding, Portuguese Bacon and, 260–261
    Quiche Lorraine, 50–51
    Salad, Viennese Bean, Bacon and, 112
    Strata, Shrimp, Bacon, Rice and, 223
Egg Noodle, Sauerkraut, and Gypsy Bacon Soup, Hungarian, 91
England, bacon history in, 2
English bacon, 7
    Bread, Cheddar and, 237
    Pie, Egg and, 55
    purchasing, 12
    and Rice Pilaf, 225
English Faggots and Split Peas, 208–209
English Roast Guinea Hens with Bacon and Mushrooms, 172

f

Faggots and Split Peas, English, 208–209
Fatback, 5, 12
Fat-to-lean ratio, 12
Feijoada, Brazilian, 158
Fennel:
    Risotto, Italian Pancetta and, 231
    Soup, German Bacon and, 89
Figs, Bacon-Wrapped, Stuffed with Almonds in Port, 259
Fish. *See also* Seafood
    Jamaican Smoked Fish, Cheese, and Bacon Salad, 111
    Salmon, Norwegian Bacon-Wrapped Broiled, 181
    Salmon, Torte, Canadian Potato, Bacon and, 182–183
    Salt Cod with Bacon and Tomatoes, Basque, 184
    Smelts, Skewered Fried Bacon and, 71

Hungarian Noodles with Bacon and Cottage Cheese, 219
Hungarian Stuffed Pork Cutlets, 154
Hungarian Venison and Bacon Ragout, 138, 140

i

Iceberg Wedges with Bacon, Blue Cheese, and Buttermilk Dressing, 101
IGourmet.com, 17
International styles of bacon, ix–x, 5–14. *See also specific countries*
Iowa Bacon and Onion Casserole Bread, 240
Irish bacon, 7, 12
Irish Colcannon, 201
Irish Hot Pot, 141
Italian Bacon and Onion Flat Bread, 244
Italian Braised Beef and Onions with Pancetta, 146
Italian Fennel and Pancetta Risotto, 231
Italian Linguine with Shrimp, Jerusalem Artichokes, and Bacon, 221
Italian Open-Face Zucchini and Bacon Omelette, 61
Italian Rabbit Stew, 135
Italian Radicchio Smothered with Pancetta, 203
Italian Roasted Turkey Breast Stuffed with Pancetta, Raisins, and Pine Nuts, 168–169
Italian Spaghetti alla Carbonara, 216
Italian Tuna, White Bean, and Bacon Salad, 108
Italy:
    curing and smoking bacon, 4
    styles of bacon in, 8, 10, 46

j

Jamaican Smoked Fish, Cheese, and Bacon Salad, 111
Japanese Bacon Tempura, 43
Japanese Braised Pork and Bacon with Chinese Cabbage, 143
Japanese Braised Pork Belly, 162
Jefferson, Thomas, 101
Jerusalem Artichokes, Shrimp, and Bacon, Italian Linguine with, 221
Jowl, 5, 12

k

Kam Man Food Products, 18
Key West Conch and Bacon Stew, 130
Krestianskiy zatrak, 70

l

Lacquered Chinese Bacon, 28
Lard fumé, 8, 42, 60, 134
Lardo, 10
Lardons, 8, 15
Lard salé, 8, 12
Lazy H Smokehouse, x, 18
Lee, Virginia, 73
Lentil:
    French Green, Salad, Bacon and, 109
    Soup, Austrian Bacon and, 90
Lentilles du Puy, 109
Lima Bean and Bacon Casserole, 127
Linguine with Shrimp, Jerusalem Artichokes, and Bacon, Italian, 221
Lion's Head, Chinese, 161
Lobster and Bacon Ragout, Bahamian, 142
Long Island Oyster and Bacon Casserole, 126
Lop yuk, 11. *See also* Chinese Bacon
Louisiana Shrimp Creole, 178
Lowcountry Shrimp and Bacon Bog, 228

m

Macaroni, Bacon, and Cheese, Swiss, 217
McArthur's Smokehouse, 18
Magnolia Grill, 257
Mail-order sources for bacon, 17–19
Maple Custard, Canadian Bacon, 262
Mariani, John, 231
Maryland Crab, Shrimp, and Bacon Chowder, 78
Mayer, Oscar F., 3
Maytag Beef and Bacon Stew, 124
Meatball, Chicken, Bacon, and Chickpea Stew, Spanish, 136–137
Meat Loaf, Jean's Best, 150
Meat Pie, Canadian, 152–153
Mencken, H. L., 245
Mexican Squash, Yam, and Bacon Soup, 95
Microwaving bacon, 15
Minnesota Wild Rice with Bacon, Almonds, and Oyster Mushrooms, 234
Mr. & Mrs. Foster's Place, 192
Mozzarella and Pancetta Pizzas, 45–46
Mozzarella di bufala, 45
Muffins, California Bacon, 251
Mushroom(s):
    - and Bacon-Stuffed Vidalia Onions, 189

S